FANATICAL
AT
LIBERTY

How Liberty Tax Service is Changing
Lives and Transforming Communities

aBM

Published by:
A Book's Mind
PO Box 272847
Fort Collins, CO 80527

Copyright © 2014 JTH Publishing, LLC
All Rights Reserved
ISBN: 978-1-939828-67-5
Library of Congress Control Number: 2014954431
Printed in the United States of America

This book is intended to record some individual Liberty Tax Service franchisees', employees', customers', and business partners' expressions of their feelings about Liberty Tax Service or document their own actions to transform their communities in "fanatical" and heart-warming ways.

These personal narratives do not carry the legal effect of management policies, promises, or verification. Rather, they are intended to share the views of individuals about what their experience with Liberty Tax Service means to them. We appreciate all of our contributors sharing their thoughts and hope that readers enjoy learning about the Liberty culture.

Testimonials appearing within this book and the individual experiences of the customers and franchisees that are contained in this book are provided by customers and franchisees. Their experiences may not necessarily be representative of all of the goods and services offered by the mentioned providers. No claim is made that these testimonials and experiences are typical of the results or quality that consumers should generally expect. Any testimonial displayed within this book is solely representative of the views of the customer or franchisee.

The trademarks, service marks, and trade names appearing herein are the property of their respective owners. They do not imply endorsement, association, sponsorship, or approval of this book or its contents.

No part of this book may be reproduced in any form without written permission from JTH Publishing, LLC
Visit www.fanaticalatliberty.com for more life-changing stories.

TABLE OF CONTENTS

Our Mission/Our Principles I

About Liberty III

Words You Need to Know V

Transforming Our Communities
   A Big Grin Fills Up My Face! 2
   Empowering Employees with Disabilities 3
   As Long as I Have Food, I Will Share 4
   How Did You Know That We Had No Food? 5
   Hiring the Homeless 5
   Cold-weather Shelter Birthday Party 6
   "Send a Friend" Pays for Medicine 7
   The Liberty Christmas Spirit 8
   Feeding the Hungry in Our Community 9
   People Come First 10
   Party in a Blizzard 11
   Liberty Tax's Coat Drive Makes Rhode Island a Warmer Place 12
   Best Promotion EVER – Discounts for Dog Food 13
   1042 Pounds of Food! 13
   A Lesson in Giving Back 14
   Eager to Support Our Community 14
   Where There is Unity, There is Always Victory 15
   Agape Love 16
   Providing Empowerment 17
   Smiles Tell the Story 17
   Helping to Support Our Community 19
   Community Incentive 19

Create Raving Fans
   Fire Destroyed the Materials… But Not Her Heart! 24
   Fanatical Customer Service! 25
   Open 24 Hours 25
   The BEST Free Return 26
   Extra Popcorn Brings in Extra Fans 27

We Keep Tissues On Every Desk 28
Tax Refund Keeps Car from Being Repossessed 29
Overcoming Extreme Obstacles 29
Fanatical Customer Cab Service 30
One Big Happy Family 31
Taking the Time to Care 31
Liberty Culture Shines Through 33
This is Fanatical! 33
The Smallest Effort is the Greatest Reward 34
The Opportunity to Make a Difference 34
I LOVE MY JOB! 35
Building Long Term Relationships 35
Fighting for My Clients 36
Fanatical Customer Service… That Is What We Do! 37
Small Gesture – Huge Impact 38
We Have the Check Already for that Sweet Family! 38
One of Our Proudest Moments 41
Restoring Faith in Good Human Beings 42
The Tenaciousness of the Liberty Tax Team 43
A Customer for Life 45

From Our Raving Fans (just a few posts from FanaticalatLiberty.com)
Liberty Rocks! 48
They Genuinely Care About Us 49
Jeweled Eagle: God Bless America 51
Without the Stress 52
NOBODY ELSE Will Do Our Taxes! 53
Fighter 53
Amazing Service! 54
Saved Thousands of Dollars 55
Fast and Easy to Understand 55
First Time Taxpayer 56
Fantastic and Very Friendly 56
Mom Didn't Raise No Fool 56
I Trust Them 57
User Friendly Website 58
Making Tax Season Less Stressful! 58
Life, Liberty, and the Pursuit of Happiness 58

Wonderful Service 59
Setting the Standard.. 60
We Were Able to Have Our Honeymoon 61
How Liberty Tax Changed Our Lives 61
Creature of Habit 62
Keep Up the Good Work!... 63
Liberty Tax Really Gets All Your Money Back....................................... 63
We are Eternally Grateful!... 64
A Healthy Refund.. 64
More Than Just a Number 65
You Guys Are Awesome! 65
Qualified Tax Professionals 66
We Love Liberty!.. 66
Liberty Helped When I Needed Them Most.. 67
I Was in a Panic!.. 67
Liberty Turned My Day Around! 68
Thank You for Helping Me 68
I Will Never Use Another Tax Prep Company!..................................... 69
You Are My Liberty Tax Family 69

Give Loyalty, Get Loyalty
God, Family, and Business 72
Liberty Gave My Heart a Chance to Heal... 73
I am a Liberty Fanatic... 75
It's Our Company 76
My Dream of Ownership... 76
Our Clients Love Us Back 77
My American Dream 78
The Greatest Place to Work.. 79
The Culture of Winning 81
Liberty Has Taken Me from Employee to Employer! 82
I Love My New Life... 83
Liberty Will Always Be a Part of My Family... 83
Surrounded by Passionate People 84
I Never Looked Back 85
God Answers Prayers, and Liberty was Part of Our Answer!....................... 86

Fanatical Wavers

365 Days Sober 90
High School Senior Loves Liberty! 91
$1000 in Cash! 92
Liberty is Everywhere! 92
Willis the Waver Makes Us #1 92
A Big Man with a Heart of Gold 93
We're a Family! 94
Fanatical Energy! 95
Waving at People, Not Cars 96
Kevin Gets His Groove On 96
Greg Epitomizes What a Waver Should Be 97
Party on Garden Grove Street 98
The Most Valuable Wavers 99
A Gleaming Personality 99
Helping Amy 100
A Reason to Get Out of Bed in the Mornings 101
True Pride and Accomplishment 101
A Brand New Person! 103
Out of My Comfort Zone 103
The Difference a Smile Can Make 104
I Love Waving to People 104
Jeremy's Message Has to be Heard 105
The Opportunity to Work 106
Blessing in Disguise 106
Finishing Strong 107
A Marriage Made in Liberty 108
Everyone Deserves a Chance 109

Family Matters

Liberty Tax and the Olympics? 112
19 February 2014 113
My Grandma's Last Hour 114
Corporate Attorney AND Mom 115
I am Changed Forever 117
Work Hard, Get Recognized, Get Rewarded 118
Baby Announcement – Maria Lucia Artese 119
Before Liberty, I Was Giving Up Hope 119
Stop and Listen 121
Time with My Son 122

 Gaining a New Family 122
 My Daughter's Guardian Angel 123
 Bringing Gizzy to Work With Me! 124

Challenge Ourselves, Challenge Each Other, Break Boundaries
 I am a Survivor 128
 51 Stores and Counting! 129
 From Homemaker to Business Owner 130
 John Saw What I Could Become 131
 Reach for Your Dreams 132
 Liberty Belles 133
 A Marine Finds Liberty 133
 Life Changing 134
 Improve Each Day, Let Go of Yesterday 136
 #1 136
 Unlimited Opportunity 137
 Enjoy the Journey 138
 Follow a Proven System 139
 It is Your Choice 139
 It's My Time to Shine 140
 Liberty Changed My Heart 141
 I Had Absolutely No Tax Knowledge 142
 I Had No Business Experience 142
 My Fanatical Story 143

Liberty Took a Chance on Me
 A Business Owner at Age 19! 146
 Life, LIBERTY, and The Pursuit of Happiness 149
 Liberty Changed My Life Forever! 150
 Liberty Gave Me a Chance 150
 Liberty Showed Up At the Perfect Time 151
 John Hewitt Believed in Me 152
 "You Have a Way with People" 154
 When You Are a Millionaire, You Can Pay for Dinner 155
 Thanks for Giving Me a Chance 157
 Liberty Gave Me a Sense of Pride 157
 I Grew Up at Liberty 158
 I Got My Big Break Through Liberty 159
 Liberty Gave Me Hope 160
 Thank You for Giving Me My Life and Self-Esteem Back 161

Liberty is the Better Job! 161
I'm Never Going Back to Manual Labor 162
The Path to Liberty! 163
University of Phoenix Scholarship Winner................................. 165
Winning a Full Tuition Scholarship 167
A Scholarship Will Change My Life... 168

Liberty Beyond Borders
The Land of the Free... 172
Bringing Smiles to Children in Mexico 173
From Cleveland to Africa 173
Giving at a New Level... 175
Letter -Lee Warren/Community Relations Manager/Stop Hunger Now.. 176
Ending World Hunger, One Country at a Time......................... 177
20/20 Vision... 178
Achieving My Dreams Through Liberty.................................... 179
The Security to Believe in Me 180

Join Our Family Business – Danny Hewitt 184

OUR MISSION

Set the standard, improve each day
and have some fun!

OUR PRINCIPLES

- Create raving fans!
- Be honest, show respect and have integrity
- Monitor results, not activities
- Mistakes are a wise person's education
- Challenge ourselves, challenge each other, break boundaries
- Give loyalty - Get loyalty
- Communication, Communication, Communication
- Attitude is a matter of choice - you make the right choice
- Enjoy the journey - do it with pride
- Contribute to the team

ABOUT LIBERTY

Founder and CEO, John Hewitt, is fanatical about taxes and unmatched customer service. A nationally recognized name in the tax return preparation and accounting world, Hewitt is a veteran of 45 tax seasons, the founder of two top tax preparation firms, and a former H&R Block Regional Director. *Accounting Today* magazine has named Hewitt one of the accounting profession's Top 100 most influential people fifteen times. The International Franchise Association honored Hewitt as its Entrepreneur of the Year in February 2006.

One of the things that makes Liberty unique is how supportive we are of our franchisees and their fanatical commitment to change the world. Culture defines Liberty and it's time for the world to know the stories of our owners, employees, partners, clients, and friends. Our tax return preparation franchise has consistently been recognized as a leader among all franchises, not just personal income tax based businesses. We have been awarded a top spot among franchises by magazines such as *Black Enterprise, Poder/Hispanic Enterprise*, and *Military Times Edge*. *Accounting Today* named Liberty Tax to its "Top Tax Firms" list 2010-2014. Liberty Tax Service has been ranked as one of the top franchise opportunities on *Entrepreneur* magazine's annual Franchise 500 every year from 1998 to 2014.

Overall, there are more than 4,400 Liberty Tax Service offices operating in the United States and Canada, where we operate as Liberty Tax Service Canada. Liberty Tax Service started in Canada on September 1, 1997 when CEO John Hewitt acquired a Canadian tax franchisor, U&R Tax Depot. In 1998, the company became Liberty Tax Service and opened five offices in the United States. Our goal is to become the #1 tax service in the universe by 2020. Culture and giving back drives that vision.

Liberty Tax Service is headquartered in Virginia Beach, Virginia. Liberty continues to expand, offering personal income tax service in an ever-growing list of locations nationwide. Experience drives every Liberty Tax franchisee, and it's experience that has made us capable of such remarkable growth in a short period of time. The knowledge of the management team and headquarters staff totals over 600 years of tax and franchise industry expertise. That's a powerful resource when it comes to developing systems, customer service, and changing the world.

WORDS YOU NEED TO KNOW

Zee
Noun
Affectionate title given to Liberty Tax franchisees.

Fanatical – fa***nat***i*cal.
Adjective
Motivated or characterized by an extreme, uncritical enthusiasm or zeal… (Dictionary.com)

Fanatical Award - fa***nat***i*cal a***ward**
Noun
$1000 check given by John Hewitt to a Zee or employee showing extreme enthusiasm, caring, or service going beyond the extra mile.

Send-A-Friend (SAF)
Noun
$50 cash, given by participating Zees to customers, for referring a friend to complete their tax return.

Liberty- Li***ber***ty
Noun
Freedom from control. Independence. Ability to create your own future. What you will experience when you visit our offices or join our team!

B2B – Business-to-business fanatical marketing, often done in costume

P2P – Person-to-person fanatical marketing, going more than the extra mile.

TRANSFORMING

OUR COMMUNITIES

TRANSFORMING OUR COMMUNITIES

A Big Grin Fills Up My Face!

By Maureen Parkhill/Zee - Tyler, TX
Fanatical Award Winner!

It was January 3rd, 2009 and our second year owning a Liberty franchise. I was experiencing the typical frustration that so many franchisees face in finding and then keeping good wavers, when two gentlemen came into the office in response to our "Get Paid to Wave" ad. As I interviewed them, I realized they shared the same address. When I asked if they were roommates, they told me they both lived in the same house along with a lot of other men. That was when I realized they were part of a county program.

After being imprisoned for alcohol and/or drug addiction-related law violations, these men spend a couple of months in a county halfway house as their last stop before they return to a hopefully productive life again. There are 32 men at the house who are expected to seek, gain, and keep employment until they are released.

Tyler's economy is made up of mostly small businesses, has no major industries, and very few large employers, so getting a job is not nearly as easy as it may sound, especially given our economic climate the last several years. I asked if there were more guys looking for a job and two big grins filled up both of their faces! And, that was the beginning of what has become a fantastic relationship between our county and Liberty Tax! The other Liberty Tax franchisee, who has been here for three years, also employs them.

For six years now, when the first of January rolls around, I simply call the counselors at the house and tell them to start sending the guys over to apply. Not only are they street dancers, but they work weekends delivering door hangers with us. They all love working here, especially when I tell them they are responsible for 60% of our new business each year. They make this aspect of running a Liberty franchise so very simple and we, in turn, are providing these men with a good place to work, a job history on their resumes, plus hope and a leg up for their futures.

I have had a few who have stayed in the area and have come back for a couple of years to work for me again during tax season. I have always been glad they would want to come back, but also a bit sad, as I wish for them full-time employment and a higher pay scale than I can afford.

But, this is the BEST part. I hear from many of them year after year. We still do some of their taxes, but many of them who have moved off or moved home call to let me know that they are still clean and sober and are becoming more and more productive citizens. That is when a big grin fills up MY face!

Empowering Employees with DisABILITIES

By Donette Darrow/Zee - Buffalo, NY
Fanatical Award Winner!

Our two Liberty Tax Service locations have made it a point, since 2006, to hire disabled workers. Almost all of our wavers have some sort of disABILITY; we write it this way to highlight their ability. For most, this is the very first job they have ever had! Imagine a 28 or 29 year old, wanting to work, but no one would give him/her the opportunity! I am very proud to say WE DO!!!

As wavers, we have had 2 autistic brothers who have been with us since 2008. Because they now have experience, they both have landed full-time jobs. We also had a man who was injured severely; shot in the head, and run over with a car. He was left for dead and now has grand mal seizures. He cannot write his name, but is the best waver ever! With a great recommendation from us, he now is employed full-time.

We had a waver and a tax preparer with spina bifida, ages 27 and 28 years old respectively. They never had jobs because no one wanted to take a chance on them. One waver cannot write her name, but both are absolutely phenomenal employees! Never late, usually at least 15 minutes early! One has been offered a full-time job delivering meds for a drug store.

These people are a gift to society - hard working, punctual, and they treat their job and their associates with the utmost respect. They enjoy coming in EVERY day, and I am so pleased, and proud, that other businesses have seen the ABILITY in each one, rather than centering on the disability. They are now hirable!!!!

As Long As I Have Food, I Will Share

By Nicole Bellenfant/Zee - Knoxville, TN

Liberty has a long-time employee, Heather Woods, who has a large personality and an equally large heart. While leading a training class before Christmas, Heather learned that one of the students who had been having a difficult time was worried about having money to go grocery shopping.

Heather, a struggling college student with two children of her own to feed, did not think twice about going home and emptying her freezer and pantry to provide this student with food for his family. This gesture was done in a quiet and dignified manner so as not to embarrass him. Heather's motto is "as long as I have food, I will share with anyone in need."

We feel that Heather, our office supervisor, embodies the spirit of Liberty: kindness when least expected, generosity to those in need, and giving beyond your comfort zone.

How Did You Know That We Had No Food?

By Sheryl Romaniuk/Zee - Washington State

The most impoverished zip code in the entire state of Washington is located in our territory. Nearly three-quarters of students at the public schools around us qualify for free or reduced lunch. The need surrounding us is great.

On December 21st, our store gave a complete turkey dinner to 100 of our neediest local families. The dinner included a 14 lb turkey, canned sides, a bag of potatoes, rolls and a pumpkin pie. Families were identified by guidance counselors at four local elementary schools. From the employees who volunteered their time, to local businesses who donated sides at reduced costs, to the service group from a nearby university who helped us prep for the big day, the turnout and support we received was remarkable. Even our local news station showed up! Nearly all the turkey dinners were picked up by the families or delivered to their homes by our volunteers.

There were a few families who did not come and whom we could not contact so these extra dinners were delivered to clients in the neighborhood. One of these clients lives just down the street from our office. When she opened her door to find our manager standing there with a box of food, she burst into tears. "How did you know?" she cried, "How did you know that we had no food?"

We hope to continue growing our partnership with local businesses so that next year, we can increase the number of Christmas meals provided to 200. We see a lot of need in our community, and though it is easy to become overwhelmed by that need, there is comfort in knowing that in a small way, we are making a difference.

Hiring the Homeless

By Felicia Bowden/Zee & Area Developer - Evansville, IN
Fanatical Award Winner for David!

Three years ago I had a waver, David Hensler, who was just awesome. He was the best I'd seen: hardworking, honest, strong faith, and clean - but homeless much of the time. He left the area after that tax season, but the next year I got him a job in Colorado, and last year he worked for a Zee in Corpus Christi.

I was friends with him on Facebook and I would always ask him to come back. This year, I did the same and it just so happened that he was out of work, out of money, out of food, and his wife had just left him. I sent him a bus ticket and $70 - enough to get food for a week and minutes on his phone.

When he arrived, I had warm clothes for him and he had made arrangements to stay at the Evansville Rescue Mission - where he had stayed before. I took him to get food (he hadn't eaten in 2 days and took him to my main office to store his "stuff" so it wouldn't get stolen at the shelter).

I took him to the Mission that night and they wouldn't let him in because he wasn't going to be in Evansville permanently. I got him dinner and took him to one of my other new offices where he stayed the night and painted for me. Within a couple days he got into the Mission.

On Christmas Eve, when it was 21 degrees, the Mission kicked him out and put him back on the street. He went to the United Caring Shelter in Evansville where he has been staying since. One of my other wavers who "came with the store" when I bought it has also been helping him - she had him over for Christmas and lets him do his laundry.

He has been working hard for us, waving and increasing visibility. He also is recruiting wavers for us at the shelters. He has the best attitude and is always "blessed" when you ask how he is. He was featured in the *Evansville Courier and Press,* the local newspaper, and told the reporter how great the people at Liberty are - hiring the homeless and taking care of them.

Cold-Weather Shelter Birthday Party

By Suzann D. Medicus/Zee, CPA - Baltimore, MD

We own Liberty Tax on the Westside of Baltimore, and are heavily involved in supporting the Westside cold-weather shelter for men. We are active participants in our church, providing weekly meals to the homeless. My husband is a chef and a group gets together each month to cook and then deliver 120 meals weekly. Also, at the beginning of the tax season, we (at Liberty) sponsor a shelter birthday party. We provide cake and ice cream for the guests of the shelter, as well as a gift card for each person whose birthday is in January.

We invite the homeless to our waver tryouts, then hire them and pay them in cash, because they often don't have IDs, so they cannot cash checks. We have been able to help some get out of the shelter by keeping them paid and by holding onto their bonus, and then using that as a deposit for a room or an apartment. They can come to our offices to warm up and to work. We have had some members of this community return year after year.

We also support a very successful internship program with the University of Maryland, Baltimore County, where I am an adjunct professor. We hire students and train them to be tax preparers. They get paid an educational stipend and also get college credit. This has been run steadily for about six years now. I believe we may have twenty interns this year. Some return another year, two, three, or four to become tax junkies.

We also are active members of the Greater Catonsville Chamber and the Southwest Baltimore Business Forum. Giving back is what this business is all about.

"Send a Friend" Pays for Medicine

By Mary Hobbs/Zee - Maryville, TN

We had a returning client send a friend to us, and first thing in the morning, we called the gal to give her the $50 SAF thank you. The phone rang and rang. She finally answered and sounded really sick.

We told her we had $50 dollars for her because she referred a friend. She almost started crying. Our client told us that she had gone to the emergency room the night before and, because she doesn't have insurance, only had money for one of her prescriptions. With the $50 dollars in cash, she was able to go to the pharmacy right away and get the rest of the medicine she needed.

She was so grateful! She told us we were a blessing. In ten years of working with Liberty Tax, we've seen many blessings, but this was a first! I'm sure she'll be sending more friends our way!

The Liberty Christmas Spirit

By Charles R. Garcia/ Zee - Houston, TX

Having acquired another franchise last year, we decided to give back in our new neighborhood. The week of Thanksgiving, and again the week of Christmas, we met with the Human Resources Advocate for Cypress Creek High School (a local high school in Houston) and arranged to have them identify families that needed assistance. We did this in my existing (Cypress) location the prior year with good results; however, the need was seen as greater at the new location.

At Thanksgiving, we gave each identified family a free turkey along with a goodie bag. We gave out about 15 turkeys at Thanksgiving.

At Christmas, it actually worked out even better as several others added to the stuff that we gave away:
- My adult daughter contributed several dozen cookies to our giveaway.
- A couple of employees wanted to help as well, so they contributed some cash, which was divided into envelopes.
- A local gas station (Raceway) was just opening up and the area director was giving all local business owners a certificate for $20 of free gas. I told him that while I appreciated the gesture, would he mind if I gave it to one of these needy families. He asked about the program and was so impressed that he gave us all remaining coupons to add to our stack. He then went to his vehicle and added several $5 manager's gift certificates for use in their convenience store.

Bottom line, during Christmas week we helped 17 families, each getting a turkey, a goodie bag (candies, t-shirt, notebook, pen, etc.), a bag of cookies, an envelope with some cash, a $20 Gas card, and a $5 coupon for the convenience store.

The response we received made us regret that we did not do more. A few broke down and cried; they were so grateful. A couple noted how this would change their Christmas. What was a minor expense to us was very significant to them. I have to say, what we received in inspiration was worth much more than the amount we spent. We all left high in the Christmas spirit.

We did not market the program, as it was our contribution to the community. While we may or may not get any of these folks to come to us, one of the high schools we supported last year promoted us. We are doing the taxes for two of their non-profit organizations. Indirectly, we have received very good press. Either way, the spiritual benefit to us was fantastic.

Feeding the Hungry in Our Community

By Frank and Jean Grim/Zee & Area Developers - VA,TX

As a Liberty Franchisee and Area Developer, we do several things that benefit the community. Every Tuesday, I drive to the food bank, pick up a substantial meat order (5-10 cases of pork, chicken, fish – whatever I'm told to do) and I deliver it to the St. Vincent's Backdoor Ministry. They feed about 130 people per day. They hope to someday build on to the church, so there would be a place where people can eat inside.

We bought a freezer for St. Vincent's because theirs broke. It's a stand up freezer instead of a chest, so the people who come in to get food to cook their own meals can now easily find whatever they need.

We also contribute (just about monthly) to St Vincent's to buy food for the food bank. Many people who go there are customers of Liberty. Some of them are between jobs or need help for another reason. We also meet once a month on Saturday and work at the food pantry at St. Kateri Tekakwitha Catholic Community Church. We put together a shopping basket for hungry families with meats, canned goods, and other donated foods.

Finally, we have a Liberty waver who became too disabled to wave. He's one step away from becoming homeless. We find him various, odd jobs. He helped me with the meat delivery, and I was able to buy him lunch. He cleans all of the Liberty offices and I pay him. Sometimes he washes cars. We do our best to help him. We feel it's important to give back to the community because the community has been so wonderful to us.

People Come First!

By Tiffany Dodson/ Area Developer - NC & TN /Zee - Asheboro, NC

Yesterday, I was finishing an employee tax return for my fourth year waver, Eddie, and his wife, Tanya, a first year marketing employee. It had been several days since we started the return because Tanya was in the hospital for over a week.

While signing, Tanya was telling me that she is so grateful that her husband started waving for us four years ago. If Eddie had not done that, then she would have not had the business to business marketing job this year, and she would be dead. She said that she had told many people how Liberty Tax saved her life.

I had a puzzled look on my face, and she explained how.

Tanya came to work a few weeks ago feeling poorly. It was the heat of peak tax season, and she knew that we needed marketing help. She came to the call center to collect supplies. Our marketing manager, Rebekka, could tell that Tanya did not feel well. After discussing what Tanya was feeling, Rebekka insisted that Tanya go to the emergency room. Rebekka told Tanya that her health was more important than peak season, and that she knew that Ryan and I (the owners) would feel the same way.

Rebekka followed Tanya to the hospital, and within 30 minutes the doctor was performing emergency surgery. He told Tanya that 30 minutes later, and she would have made Eddie a widow, and left their two children without a mother.

Tanya had her appendix removed and a section of her colon/intestines removed. Needless to say, Ryan, Rebekka, and I are also grateful that Tanya and her family are happy and healthy today. She rejoined us in the call center on President's Day. And I am so very proud of our marketing manager, Rebekka, who knows that people come first!

Liberty is also changing many lives in Asheboro, NC, a small rural town of 18,000 with unemployment rumored in the low 20% range. This year, Liberty hired 15% of everyone who interviewed for a position at the local Goodwill Job Services Center. Fifty-two people interviewed, eight were hired for tax preparers, business to business, and waver positions.

Whether it's saving lives or changing families, Liberty is bringing hope to our community, one person at a time.

Party in a Blizzard

By Jenny Moreland/Zee - Atlanta, GA

At the end of January, as most people saw on the news, it started snowing in Atlanta. We called it "Snow-pocolyspe!" This is very uncommon in Atlanta and it was a mess because a lot of people were sent home from work or school, all at the same time. We had traffic jams all across the city.

We decided not to send anyone home, but to stay and have a roadside party! We set up our barbeque and cooked some hot dogs. All of our wavers were out and they were having a great time in the snow. We took the opportunity to pass out coupons and goodie bags to the drivers that were stuck on the street in front of us.

We also did our best to help people. One of our return customers was having her taxes done and got stuck. She was terrified of driving in the snow and it turns out she lives not too far from me. I'm from Ohio, so I have some experience driving in snowy conditions. I told her I would give her a ride home. It took us six hours to get there, but I kept my promise! We had to walk together the last mile, but she was very grateful to have someone with her.

When the snow crisis calmed down, many of the customers remembered us and came back to have their taxes done. The Blizzard of Atlanta turned into a bonus for Liberty, and a great way to shine!

Liberty Tax's Coat Drive Makes Rhode Island a Warmer Place

By Paul Pliakas/Zee - Providence, RI

In January, Rhode Island Liberty Tax locations participated in a "Stuff the Bus" Coat Drive with the Providence Bruins, and RIPTA (Rhode Island Public Transit Authority) to benefit the Providence Corps of the Salvation Army.

Coat collections began on January 2 at participating Liberty offices across Rhode Island, and continued through Friday January 24th, culminating at a Providence Bruins game at the Dunkin' Donuts Center – where we presented the coats to the Salvation Army in a RIPTA bus.

Liberty's Marketing Department created a full-color flyer for the event, at the request of Zee, Steve DeMedeiros, and Steve distributed it to all the Liberty Zees in Rhode Island. Zees posted the Coat Drive flyer on their early season business-to-business marketing calls to show their Rhode Island neighbors and customers that Liberty Tax loves to give back to the community.

Both the Providence Bruins (the American Hockey League affiliate of the Boston Bruins) and RIPTA were key supporters of the Coat Drive, promoting the event with a combination of press releases, Facebook, and web postings. The local Salvation Army Corps Commander told us he was more than thrilled when we brought the idea for the Coat Drive to him.

It's been cold in Rhode Island this winter, and the "Stuff the Bus" Coat Drive collected 244 coats for the local Salvation Army Citadel. The "Stuff the Bus" Coat Drive is just one more example of how Liberty Tax gives back to local communities throughout the country!

Best Promotion EVER
- Discounts for Dog Food

By Alyce Copeland/Zee - Sierra Vista & Benson, AZ

We were looking for a great community promotion after early peak. We decided to give a $50 discount for donating a 20-pound or larger bag of dog or cat food for the local animal shelters and rescue leagues. It became so popular and effective that we have continued it through the end of March.

To date, we have donated approximately 200 bags of pet food plus dog cookies, toys, cat litter, etc. to the Border Animal Rescue, Tombstone Animal Shelter, Huachuca City Animal Shelter, Sierra Vista Animal Shelter, and the Benson Animal Shelter. We even had a spread, including pictures, in our local newspaper and a radio announcement provided by Border Animal Rescue.

1042 Pounds of Food!

By Bill McPherson/Zee - Apopka, FL

At my Liberty Tax location, I know that hundreds of people go hungry every day because it is a lower income area, so I decided to do a food drive with the 2nd Harvest Food Bank.

I made a huge goal of collecting 1040 pounds of food. When I made the goal, I thought it was a huge number, but as time went on the amount of food we received was amazing! We had so much food in our office, people starting asking if they could have some because they needed food. When I heard this, I told my employees if anyone said this they could go to the store next door and buy some food for those people.

I called the 2nd Harvest Food Bank and told them that we needed a pick up and they came with a small truck and realized that they had to bring a larger truck to pick it up. They were amazed! When they weighed the collection, we had collected 1042 pounds of food! I know we made a difference in Apopka!

A Lesson in Giving Back

Amanda Sweeney/Marketing Manager - Staunton, VA

This year, we rode the trolley several days at the beginning of the season and I learned that they now charge 25 cents per person per ride. It doesn't seem like a lot of money, but I learned that it has affected the daily riders. So my little girl, Kitana, and I decided to grab a couple rolls of quarters and pay for everyone's ride the next couple of times we rode.

Everyone appreciated the gesture, and I was able to teach my daughter a lesson in giving back!

Eager to Support Our Community

Mark Mihalka/Zee - Pittston, PA

This year, we had our 7th Annual Liberty Tax Charity Golf Tournament on May 24th.

Over the years, our tournaments have raised money for the March of Dimes, A Little Bit of Home (making care packages for Marines), the Redmond Education Fund (local family that lost their father unexpectedly at age 40), the Zawierucha Family (a family that lost their father in an ATV accident), and last year we raised over $13,000 dollars for Breast Cancer Awareness in honor of Barb Sciandra (a local mother of 3, diagnosed with breast cancer).

This year, our tournament raised money for Melanoma Awareness in honor of Rosemary Bilbow Manbachi (family member that most recently won the battle with melanoma and wants to help others with the same diagnosis).

We just like to let everyone know that after April 15th we are active and are eager to support our community!

Where There is Unity, There is Always Victory

By David Perez/Manager - Harlingen, TX

On January 23, 2014 there was an unfortunate tragedy where a fire destroyed an apartment complex where one of Liberty's team members, Kris, lived. Thankfully, his apartment was saved and no one was injured, but the fire did destroy many personal belongings and displaced six families who lived there. Once our office found this out, we knew that it was our duty to help out these families in a time of need. Kris and our team had a meeting immediately and coordinated a fundraising event for these  families within 48 hours. Kris and our general manager personally met with each family to find out what they needed. A list was made and it all took off from there. Our team contacted all of our local marketing partners and gathered donations to help out the families in need.

On January 25, 2014 Liberty Tax hosted a roadside party benefit and invited the community to attend. We contacted the local news crew to come out and do a live remote to get publicity. We collected clothes, baby  items, furniture, and non-perishable items. One of our partners donated hotel rooms for the families to stay for a week and another donated food for every family for the entire week. There were lines of cars around the parking lot of our office with people dropping off box after box of donations. The turnout was so good that we rented a storage unit to keep all of the items to divide and distribute to the families. Our staff volunteered to drive these families to and from the storage unit, and even hand delivered special items. We also offered free tax preparation for all six families.

Our Liberty Team came through for all those who were affected by this tragedy. We still continue to support these families as much as possible. Kris and our team made this a memorable event and showed how important it is to help others.

Agape Love

By Liz McEwan/Franchise Development
Representative - Virginia Beach, VA

I am a youth group director of a small church in Virginia Beach. I began my youth leadership with this church in September of 2013, but was hired as a youth director in January of 2014. When I started leading the youth, we only had one kid that came on Sunday nights. This was so heart breaking because there are kids that attend the church but they were not involved in the youth program. Once I was hired, I was able to reach out to kids that attended my church, but did not go to the youth program. We immediately built up our base from one youth to about six, but my goal was 15 kids in three months. It has been four months and we now have over 23 kids each week! It grew so much.

One of the reasons I believe that it grew was our focus on mission work. In January, our kids made over 75 Agape Bags for homeless people in Hampton Roads. These are bags that are to give to the homeless when you see them on the side of the road while driving. The bag's contents include- water bottle, socks, soap, beef jerky, a razor, crystal light lemonade, a Bible verse, and directions to my church, as well as hours for our food pantry. My youth made these bags with love and were thrilled at how many lives we could touch.

After about two months we have given out over 100 bags to local homeless people who absolutely adore the contents of the bag. Each week- almost daily - one of my youth kids call me to tell me about someone they touched with the Agape Bag that day.

I understand, because when I was driving to Liberty Tax, my first day on the job, I was able to give two homeless men a bag to help care for their needs. They were so grateful. Today, I passed one of the men that I gave a bag to a few weeks ago and he flagged me down at a stoplight with a huge smile on his face. He lifted his jeans to show me that he was wearing the socks we gave him and, with a grin, he said- John 3:16!

Each of my youth kids has stories such as these. It's amazing how Agape love spreads throughout our community. We are making 200 bags next weekend, and are looking forward to fanatically giving these bags to those who are most deserving.

Providing Empowerment

Karen Tolley/Zee - Cambridge and Church Creek, MD

I was born and raised on the Eastern Shore, and I'm no stranger to helping this community. After graduating locally, I was asked to be Treasurer of my small township 19 years ago. That started a sincere interest in creating and passing policy for sound government. Since 1997, I've been Town Commissioner, representing the area on several community councils/committees. Owning and operating a Liberty Tax Franchise seemed like a natural extension of my community outreach.

Besides being able to provide local residents with a paycheck, we provide empowerment. The skills that returning employees learn, season to season, benefits them in all areas of their life. Working with clients directly fine-tunes and hones customer service skills, reviewing tax returns teaches analytical skills, and being entrusted with handling confidential data and personal finance instills honesty and integrity. Low-income clients and students also benefit from nearly 100 free annual tax returns, tax school, and seminars throughout the year.

As a CPA, I represent many tax clients before the IRS and State at a significantly reduced rate or most often FREE. The first correspondence (which clears up 90% of most issues) is always FREE. Why? Because I want FANATICAL customers to let us do what we do BEST!

Smiles Tell the Story

By Samantha Slapnik/Zee - Myrtle Beach, SC

Myrtle Beach, South Carolina, known as the Grand Strand for its long stretch of coastline is, without a doubt, a tourist town. With only about 30,000 "locals," our city has a lot of amenities thanks to the hospitality industry, but is really just a small town at heart. Our office is located in an inland suburb of Myrtle Beach, known as Carolina Forest.

On March 17, 2013, a spark ignited a massive fire in our small community. Thanks to dry conditions, high winds, and dated fire codes, the flames spread quickly, engulfing an entire condo community within minutes. The Windsor Green Condos are located just one mile from our office. In all, 26 buildings and 108 units were destroyed leaving dozens of families homeless.

In the days following the fire, the community rallied with fundraisers and donations of clothing and household goods. Our office served as a drop-site for donations and our employees gathered carloads of personal items to help replace some of what the fire stole from these families. Despite these efforts, it didn't seem like we were doing enough. These clients are our friends. I've known many of them for years. We've watched their children grow up.

While I considered donating funds to the Red Cross, I really wanted to focus on the families we serve. So I scoured our client list, identifying by address, the seven clients who lived in what once was Windsor Green. I called each one, offering our sympathies asking, "How can we help?" In the following conversations, I heard terrifying stories of that knock on the door, screams to "Get Out!" and the surreal get-away as they watched their lives go up in flames. Knowing the tough months ahead, and hoping I didn't offend anyone, I offered to refund their tax preparation fees from that year. We prepared packets for each client, including copies of their tax return, picture IDs, social security cards and a check.

One by one, each client came in to pick up the packet. There were two families; one was a cousin to the other who had just moved to the beach so their kids could grow up together. There was one college-age kid, wondering how he would be able to graduate in May without clothes, books and a car. There was an older couple, who had spent years building a life they could enjoy in retirement. With hugs and tears, we offered to help in any way we could.

In the off-season, I got calls and visits from several of these clients, asking for information, job opportunities or just checking in. The older couple came in several times, each visit more heart breaking than the last. Miss Helen and her husband, Bill, are picture-perfect southerners. He always pulled out her chair to sit and held her hand. She always wore a warm smile and a butterfly barrette in her hair. But in the months after the fire, her smile faded. When she came in, we talked and hugged, but she just wasn't the same. She said she felt lost. They'd consolidated their lives when they moved here from North Carolina, keeping only what meant most – pictures and mementos of a well-lived life. Now, it was all gone.

As Tax Season 2014 began, I wondered about our Windsor Green families. The condos were being rebuilt and were set to re-open in February. Luckily, I didn't have to wonder long. Over the next few weeks, all seven of those clients came back, and when they did it was a party. With hugs and a grand entrance, each one greeted us like family. The cousins had relocated to houses just a few blocks from each other. The college-age kid graduated, and is now engaged to be married. And when Miss Helen came back, her smile told the story. They had moved back into Windsor Green, and outfitted a new life – including several new butterfly barrettes to adorn her hair.

Helping to Support Our Community

Jeff Martin /Customer & Traffic Reporter
for a local radio station - Pompano Beach, FL

I sent the following to a contest in a local magazine to recognize a company that gives back to the community. Liberty Tax epitomizes service and giving back to the community and is deserving of the award:

To Whom it May Concern,

Saw the contest in *Pompano Today* magazine and would like to nominate Liberty Tax Service of Pompano Beach. It is ironic that my relationship began with them by winning a free tax prep at an Adopt a Pet event that they donated to the event. They are now my full time tax accountants.

For 10+ years- Liberty Tax Service (two locations in Pompano Beach) has been heavily involved in the community supporting events and fundraising efforts through the Pompano Rotary Club, Relay for Life, Horses for Heroes, Unity in the Community, and the Pompano Beach Chamber of Commerce, among others. You see them at many city and community events with Statue of Liberty costumed staff handing out Liberty crowns and adding to the fun. They have also sponsored two softball teams. Liberty gives back to the community through marketing programs. Instead of buying advertising from national firms, Liberty spends nearly its entire marketing budget using local individuals for grassroots marketing. Many are people who are unemployed, are not able to work fulltime or just starting their first job. In turn, their paychecks are then spent at other local businesses. So when you see the Statue of Liberty out in front of their office, remember that he or she is out there helping to support our community!

Community Incentive

Judouane Lazarre/ Zee - West Hempstead, NY

We have worked hard over the past tax season in the community we service. In March 2013, we invited the West Hempstead senior art class students to paint a mural of Lady Liberty in our office. We were able to have students, their families and school staff visit. In addition, we donated $1,000.00 to the school's art program.

On November 16, 2013 our Liberty Tax Service office located at 124 Hempstead Turnpike, West Hempstead, hosted our first annual free turkey drive. This initiative was a way of introducing ourselves to the community and giving back during a time of thanks. On that day, we were able to give away 60 free premium turkeys to clients, community members and members of the West Hempstead Chambers of Commerce. We celebrated with so much joy and laughter and were happy that we were giving back. Our staff joined in as well, by bringing some of their family members. We are proud to have been able to achieve our goal of providing service to the community as well as acquiring new clients.

CREATE RAVING FANS

Fire Destroyed the Materials... but not her heart!

By Stacy Hausenfluck/Customer - Stephens City, VA

(Cathy Anderson, Liberty Office Manager, is a Fanatical Award winner!)

In the afternoon of March 10, 2014, a fire broke out at the dry cleaners right next to the Liberty Tax in Stephens City, VA. The blaze caused extensive damage to Festival Cleaners and smoke damage to Liberty Tax. The entire strip mall was evacuated and most of the employees went home, traumatized. However, there was one dedicated employee that never left the building. I would like to nominate Cathy Anderson, our Office Manager, for the outstanding customer service award.

Dedication is defined as "devotion: the quality of being devoted or committed to something," and Cathy is the true definition of dedication when it comes to Liberty Tax. Even though much of the building was covered in black soot, Cathy showed up every day with a positive attitude and the heart to keep that office running smoothly. Since the building was quarantined until the Fire Marshall could inspect and reopen it, Cathy sat on the sidewalk for days helping to prepare taxes and file refunds. She endured the cold and the complaints and still stood strong by Liberty's side. She did all of this, without being asked! In my eyes, that is true customer service excellence.

To top it off, when the building did reopen, she worked 12+ hour days to get the business back in the swing of this (it was in the heart of tax season). After a week of 60+ hours, she was closing one night when a middle-aged gentleman walked in asking her to prepare his taxes. It was 4 minutes to closing and she had been there since 9 AM. He explained that he needed his taxes completed so he can get the $50.00 cash to feed his family. Cathy did not hesitate to log her computer back on and prepare his taxes. She put her exhaustion aside and happily committed her time to him. Again, showing the definition of true dedication.

Liberty Tax is not just a place of employment for Cathy it is her extended family and she, beyond a doubt, deserves this award!

Fanatical Customer Service!

By Ritu Khadiya/Zee - Santa Clarita, CA

I want to share with you a fanatical customer service story! Last year, I saw a client stand in our doorway with a big box of paperwork. She would not come in and was crying on the doorstep. We finally persuaded her to come in and she told us the story of her life.

Her name is Jo, and she is a special needs teacher in our local school. Previously, she had a business with her husband and let's just say that "life" happened to her. She ended up getting a letter from the IRS for a $750,000 penalty!

We had three of my best preparers and bookkeepers working on this, and on her returns. Today, finally, we received word that her penalties were reduced to nothing and her wages will not be garnished! We solved this problem by doing her taxes correctly, and talking her through this. We didn't even have to go with her to the IRS office.

Ever since the first day we met Jo, we have been like a second home to her. We made a commitment to help her through all of this. One of our preparers, Violeta Carmen Baxter, also has kids in the local schools and Joanne has referred more than 15 clients to her and our office.

Sometimes fanatical customer service begins with a simple act of kindness and the willingness to hold someone's hand.

Open 24 Hours

Vanessa Dickens/Zee - Baltimore, MD

We have 4 offices in the Baltimore area and we decided to keep one of our offices open 24 hours. We are down the street from Johns Hopkins Hospital, so we have a lot of people who work the night shift. I have many nursing friends who work late. There are also some restaurants that are open late into the night. When customers notice that we're open, we just ask them the simple question, "Have you done your taxes yet?"

We actually did one return at 4:30 a.m. Yes, that's AM! I also get phone calls all night. People can't believe that we're actually open 24 hours, so we post on Facebook to let people know that we're actually there.

Our fanatical customer service is definitely our competitive advantage. Not just the hours. We have our hot dog carts going, meatballs, and chili. So when people come into our office we make them feel very comfortable. Our staff believes in "having some fun" everyday.

Most of all, we listen. In the mornings, with our staff, we go over how we can improve everyday – 24/7.

The BEST Free Return!

Maureen Parkhill/Zee - Tyler, TX
Fanatical Award Winner!

Last week, a woman came in to do her tax return for 2012 and 2013. She told our preparer that she still owed the IRS $711 for 2011. She had not done her 2012 return because she was afraid she would owe money and she just could not deal with it. She also told our preparer that her daughter and son-in-law had moved in with them over a year ago, and her husband was quite ill and had not worked much. All of this was putting a tremendous amount of stress on her.

Surprisingly, she and her husband were getting a $1300+ refund for 2013. She told our preparer that she could not afford to pay very much for each of these returns. She left to go to work at Dillard's across the street from our office.

Our preparer came to me to ask what we should do. I mulled the situation over and decided to do both returns for free. The 2013 refund would come very, very close to covering the 2011 and 2012 debt to the IRS if not wiping it clean. That way, the stress of owing the IRS would not continue to hang over their heads. I called her at work and told her what we were going to do. She started crying, thanked me, and said she would be in after work.

When she came in, she pulled me aside. She began thanking me again, crying, and then told me something that was gut wrenching. Their 4-month-old granddaughter had died 3 weeks before. She told me that doing these taxes for free made her feel that maybe there was hope. That perhaps this was a sign that they all would survive and life would be okay one day.

When I made that decision to do both returns for free I had two motivations. One was, of course, why we do free returns - so that we gain a paying client next year and create raving fans. My much stronger motivation was just to help someone climb out of a hole with the IRS. At the time I made the call, I had no idea what this family had been through and how much a small act of kindness could mean. I think in the seven years we have been doing this, that was the BEST free return we have ever done!

Extra Popcorn Brings in Extra Fans

By Tena Meermans /Zee - South Carolina

Customer service is one of the keys to success. My husband and I, as the owners, make sure we take an active role and personally work as the receptionist and greeters. At the end of the day, when we clean up the popcorn machine, I make it a point to take some of the extra popcorn to the gas station workers (who are stuck working until midnight). I tell them that we're from Liberty Tax and this is a little treat for them. They are so appreciative!

This has been so successful, that we started making extra popcorn bags during the day when we are slow. We take these to workers at Waffle House and other businesses, along with coupons stapled to the bag. That's in addition to the cookies and other goodies we give away doing business to business marketing. The workers all love it!

From tax preparers to wavers, our entire staff gets involved with marketing. We actually get in costumes ourselves to teach our wavers how to create raving fans. We hired one of the University of South Carolina cheerleaders, and it's hard to get any work done when he's out there. He's fabulous and fun to watch!

A smile and an upbeat demeanor are the most important things for customer service. One client said this is the first time she actually felt like tax preparers cared what her name was. That brought tears to my eyes. If you truly care about the customers and their needs, they will see it and that will make all the difference.

We Keep Tissues On Every Desk

By Rachel Portnoy Bradley/Zee - Hillsboro, OR

The client "Ms. Smith," (not married and not her real name) came in for a double check on her return, just like one of our competitor's promises. She had just come from this other tax preparer. They called her in because she owed money and she didn't have it. She was barely making ends meet as it was. This other tax group told her that her kids had to live with her all 12 months for her to get any credits, which as anyone who has taken the awesome Liberty Tax School knows, is not the case.

Every year, her three children live with her during the school year from late August through early June. The summers are spent split between Dad, Grandma, and various summer camps, if Mom can get them in for free. There was no Form 8332 (Release of Claim to Exemption) and I offered to help them file one just to make sure, but even a conservative estimate gave Mom at least nine months caring for her kids.

Of course, knowing that another tax store denied her the right to any credits, I made sure we did our due diligence. We made thorough notes for our files and copies of all the documents we needed. In the end, we determined that she was fully eligible to claim all three children: Head of Household status, Exemptions @ $3900, Child Tax Credit @ $1K, and the maximum Earned Income Credit available.

She started crying when I showed her the refund.

And THAT'S why we keep tissues on every desk.

Tax Refund Keeps Car from Being Repossessed

By Mark and Camelia Adel/Zees - Pinehurst, NC

A client returned to us after a difficult year, having been one of many people laid off when a local carpet plant, located just down the street from our office, closed last January. We reached out to those workers and offered to prepare their tax returns for free last year. She was one of many who came back to us this year.

This client had endured a difficult year, finding only part time work here and there. Plus, with unemployment and a lump sum distribution from the closed business, she fully expected to owe money to the IRS and the State of North Carolina. At that time, she was also in jeopardy of losing her car since she had not been able to keep up the payments, and it was about to be repossessed.

As we worked through her taxes, it became clear that this would not be the case. In fact, she was going to receive a fairly substantial refund from both federal and state returns. She was so overcome by the realization that she was going to be able to keep her car - that she clearly needed in order to continue working - she completely broke down crying and hugging everyone in the office.

Helping clients like this is always a great feeling!

Overcoming Extreme Obstacles

By Angela Lovelady/Customer Service - San Diego, CA

I am here to tell you an amazing story about overcoming extreme obstacles and still delivering top-notch customer service in the process.

It all started on January 15, 2014 around 10:00 pm. The owner, Reggie Reyes, received a phone call from the Lemon Grove Fire Department. Turns out, the internal roof sprinkler system had deployed due to corrosion in the piping. The entire office was flooded: the main office, the manager's office, and the call center.

To make matters worse, the very next night, we experienced another flood. The office next door had their sprinkler system deploy. Since that office was uphill from us, the water flowed right into our office and flooded us once AGAIN!

For insurance purposes we did not move anything around in the office after the first flood, so the second flood made it nearly impossible to salvage any of our supplies.

But did that stop us? No, it did not. We are dedicated to our customers and we weren't going to let this stop us from giving the best possible customer service. Luckily, the processor was in the manager's office and on a small stand so the water did not get into the computer. We grabbed that computer, a canopy, a few tables, and set up shop in the parking lot right outside the office. We had coolers full of beverages and snacks for the customers.

The lead tax preparer for our office, Dawn Hedgecoth, was working with the Manager, Michelle Helmer, to deliver excellent customer service. The most amazing part of this whole thing was that Dawn and Michelle were not only doing taxes all day in the heat, they were also fixing up the office on their own. They cleaned the office, organized the furniture, painted the walls, retiled the bathroom, and salvaged as much as possible. They did all of that after giving 100% to their customers.

Everyday, for 10 days, we did the same thing out in the parking lot. Regardless of the circumstances, this office went above and beyond to give our customers the best service possible. Thanks to our great customers, as an office we are up 54% from where we were last year. Nothing was going to stop us from making this a great season.

Fanatical Customer Cab Service

Richard Weisenberg/Zee - Casa Grande, AZ

One of our customers recently picked up their tax refund check and went to a national retailer to get their check cashed. The customer then called our office stating they could not get it cashed, and the store was having system difficulties.

The customer called our office - very upset - because she just spent her last few dollars on cab fare getting to the store with her family, and they were stuck without any cab fare to get home. I had one of my staff members go to that store and provide them cab fare, not just to get home, but also fare for the next day so she could get back to the store to get their check cashed.

The customer was so appreciative of our fanatical customer service and plans on using us for many more years to come.

One Big Happy Family

Monique Woodson/Office Manager - Pittsburgh, PA

This is my second year working for franchise owner, Carl Marbury, at the LTS office in Mt. Oliver, PA. The past year was a year of learning and personal growth that I didn't know I was being groomed for.

As the summer came around and I was promoted to Office Manager, I started noticing that I was given challenges that were fun to meet. As we began our second season, I was truly amped with some of the new things we were going to bring to our office - from helping with the Affordable Care Act to helping customers who have offsets.

This season, we have had the opportunity to help several customers truly understand their current debt situation and help many lower their debt, get rid of their debt, or begin to make payments on their debt. Our customers have been so shocked with the results we have gotten them, and I truly feel like we are one big happy family here in Mt. Oliver.

Taking the Time to Care!

By Caleb Myles/Company Store Area Developer

Despite our best efforts, the "Vast Majority" of our Company Stores do not have customers lined up around the building, waiting to get their tax returns completed. The anecdote below, however, could certainly change that.

Doing the right thing is not always the easy thing to do. Rarely, is it convenient. But doing the right thing, especially when no one is looking, can have the power to define who we are. It can define us as individuals. It can define us as a company.

On 3/10/14, Nicole Hammond, a 1st year Liberty tax preparer in Billings, Montana didn't have any customers in the office. Instead of talking on the phone, posting on Facebook, or using this free time for her own personal gain, Nicole was using this time to call prior year customers who had not yet filed.

When Nicole reached a Mrs. Carolyn Bratlie, Mrs. Bratlie told Nicole that she was recently widowed and she has moved into an assisted living facility. Mrs. Bratlie had relied on her late husband to do their taxes but "Now that he is gone," she said, "I didn't know what to do with our taxes."

Nicole, without asking and on her own time, drove out to the nursing home to meet with Mrs. Bratlie. Nicole reviewed the process thoroughly with Mrs. Bratlie and obtained the necessary documents. Nicole stayed with Mrs. Bratlie for a while just to visit, talk, and spend some time with her. She took Mrs. Bratlie's documents back to the LTS office and worked on them there.

Once completed, Nicole drove back out to see Mrs. Bratlie to give her the completed return. Nicole explained what had been done with her taxes and what to expect moving forward. Mrs. Bratlie got a bit emotional when Nicole returned and it certainly wasn't because her taxes were complete. It was because someone took the time to notice her, to listen, to help, to validate her. She wasn't treated like a patient or a number. To Mrs. Bratlie, Nicole was someone who cared. She was her friend.

Before leaving again, Mrs. Bratlie told Nicole how thankful she was for her and that she would call us every year to do her returns. In addition, neither Nicole nor the office supervisor reached out to me to let me know any of this was happening. It was only after the call center contacted Mrs. Bratlie that I learned of what was going on. Nicole didn't do this for recognition or a raise. Nicole helped Mrs. Bratlie because she is a good person with a kind heart.

A raving, fanatical fan was certainly made. It wasn't $50 cash. It wasn't a free return. It was so much more than great customer service. It was taking the time to listen. It was taking the time to care. It was doing the right thing – even when no one was looking.

Thank you, Nicole for all that you do for Liberty Tax Service.

Liberty Culture Shines Through

By Ralph Guisti/Zee - MA

A client came into my store during first peak (we'll call him Bill). First thing he said was, "I just went to H&R Block and they wanted $99 to do my tax return... Do you believe that?" I said, "No, that's a great deal!" We discussed his tax situation and I told him that I'd never be the $99 guy, but this year I'd do it for less than Block to show him the difference.

He agreed and I had a great time discussing his job as a Coke delivery truck driver, which he held for 10 years or so. He had his taxes done by "Tanya Does Taxes"---- (no lie) for the past several years for $40. I found "Tanya" had not claimed his MA rental deduction for the past 10 years, which was about $150 for each of those 10 years.

We discussed his Coke delivery job and I asked him if the Coke drivers are rivaled by the Pepsi drivers, like in the old commercials. He laughed and said that he knew them all and they were all friends (weird). I finished the return and encouraged him to try us again next year. He said, "I'll be back."

A week went by and a client came in asking for Bill's return copy. I asked who he was and he said Bob, Bill's brother, and that Bill had passed away. I was shocked, to say the least, he was just in my store a week ago! I told him how sorry I was and that his brother seemed like a great guy. We discussed what needed to be done to release the paperwork and he thanked me and left.

A week later Bob came in with his own tax paperwork. He told me he'd been using the same tax pro for many years now, but his brother Bill had spoken so highly of us, that he wanted to give us his business. We discussed Bill as I did his taxes and we finished and parted. It's great to know that we can have such a positive impact on those around us - even in the face of a loss so great - the Liberty Culture shines through.

This is Fanatical!

AlAnn Feldmann/ Zee - Dry Ridge, KY

We had a newly married couple who came in last year. We sat down with them and explained all the ins and outs of doing a tax return. Then we surprised them and did it for free.

This year when they came in, they told us we really helped them a lot and thanked us for all our help. They discussed it and decided that they would come here for five years, no matter where they lived to "thank" us. And it was a paid return this year. They travelled 50 miles, this year, back to our office. This is Fanatical!

The Smallest Effort is the Greatest Reward

By Kathy Gordon/Tax Preparer - Billings, MT

We have a client who is elderly and needed to get her taxes done. She called the office and one of my gals, Nicole, answered that call. This client was very concerned about how she was going to get her tax return completed this year. Our client had just lost her husband and had to move to a retirement home, and also lost her license to drive, as well.

All during the past year, Nicole let her know that she didn't have to worry. We would go to her and pick up her information and once her return is completed, we'd bring back her completed return.

Nicole returned and spent some time with this client, and the client began to cry and show some emotion over all she had been through in the past year. This client was so pleased to know that we will go to her every year that we need to and is going to refer Liberty to anyone else that needs us to go to them, as well.

Sometimes the smallest effort is the greatest reward.

The Opportunity to Make a Difference

Charles Walker/Tax Preparer - Lexington, SC

I recently had an opportunity to help one of my former students and his mother in a way that changed their lives for the better. The former student was a young man I had mentored in homeroom. After talking with him, I discovered that his mother was disabled. He said she never filed taxes because she was on disability. He asked if he could claim his brother because he contributed a great deal to his support. I called the student's mother and had her come in for an interview. She explained that she had not filed taxes since going on disability in 2009.

At that time, she had consulted another tax preparer and they had told her she did not have to file. I talked with Mr. Slaughter (Zee for this office) about the situation and he explained that if she received W-2 income as a result of her disability, it was considered earned income and she could receive EIC (Earned Income Credit). She had saved her paperwork and sure enough she was eligible for EIC. I explained the situation to her and we filed her returns for 2011, 2012, and 2013.

She was so excited because she needed the money to repair her teeth and have a hip replaced. She called the office when she received her checks to let us know they had arrived. She was praising the Almighty and Liberty Tax Service. I appreciate the opportunity to make a difference.

I LOVE MY JOB!

Sharon King/Office Supervisor - Omaha, NE

I love giving Fanatical customer service to All of my clients! I make sure to always learn as much as possible about each one of them, including remembering their name and if they have filed here years before. They all have wonderful stories and just want to be heard!

I give great advice on the returns I do for them, and give future advice on how to make it better next year! I believe as a tax preparer, it's my job to help give as much information as possible! I LOVE MY JOB!!!!!

Building Long Term Relationships

By Karen Gann/Multi-Office Manager - Dallas, TX

I met Mr. Hight nine years ago when I worked for "the competition." He had always prepared his own taxes but had a question that year and stopped by my Walmart kiosk, seeking advice. His wife had just passed away, and what started as a question turned into a relationship. I have prepared his taxes every year since then, regardless of what company I worked for or where he lived. For the last several years, he mailed me his information because he lived three hours outside of Dallas.

In March of 2013, he called to tell me he had been diagnosed with Stage 4 cancer and only had weeks to live. He also told me that he would have all his paperwork in order and was adamant that I prepare his final tax return. He indicated that he would have his daughter contact me. She called me in September to let me know her father had died.

A couple of weeks ago, Mr Hight's daughter called to let me know she had all of his paperwork together and was ready to discuss her father's final tax return. It was obviously a difficult conversation and although I had known him for 10 years, she shared with me some additional insights. She told me that he had a hard time trusting people, but once he developed a relationship, he was fiercely loyal. She conveyed that her father had a keen intuition and what that said about me, my character, and my abilities as a tax professional.

To me, this is what Fanatical Customer Service means - building long-term relationships, doing whatever it takes, one customer at a time.

Fighting for My Clients

By Misty Miller/Tax Preparer - Joplin, MO

As a tax preparer, being with the public has always been a pleasure for me. I take pride in helping clients with whatever issues, dealing with their taxes that may come up. I have had my own business for 20 years and for the last two seasons, I have been a part of the Liberty family. I am the kind of person who will fight for my clients, help them get the best return that I can get them. I believe in quality work instead of quantity. If it takes two hours to do a return then I take pride that once that client leaves my office, they are happy or at least relieved knowing that we did everything that we could for them.

I have had people come from eight hours away because they needed someone to help them with six years of taxes. One was so overwhelmed, she did not know what to do. Once we were finished and she realized that she was getting a refund for most of those years, she was so excited. She said that she just needed the right person to sit her down, explain everything and basically make her see that what she was doing each year was the correct way for her. She went back to Iowa and told all her friends about her experience. I was proud of myself and knew that her word of mouth was worth the world to me.

I love to teach others and make them see that no matter how many years you have been in this business, you do learn something that you may not have known before.

I will go out of my way to help anyone, even if they cannot afford to pay me. I feel it is better to help them get caught up then to make them pay when you know that they cannot afford it. The Lord has blessed me with the ability to help others and that is my reward in life.

Fanatical Customer Service.... That is What We Do!

By Debra Teseniar/Tax Preparer - Lexington, SC

Fanatical Customer Service.... that is what we do! You have heard the saying, "neither rain, nor sleet, nor snow, nor dark of night?" I want to nominate Larry Slaughter, and many of his employees for fanatic customer service in Lexington, Redbank and Irmo, South Carolina. While snow might deter some from going to work, Larry had many employees braving the conditions with 4-wheel drives and good old (as Larry called it) Yankee tenacity for getting to the stores during sleet, snow, and freezing icy road conditions to make sure our customers got the checks that were just coming through from the first wave of processing.

In a small strip mall on a Friday night, I was the only store open. As the bright lights from our store window blazed thru the winter storm like a lighthouse on a rocky coast guiding our customers in, through the blowing snow I could see my waver boldly going where no man has ever gone.... with flashlight in hand, music in his ears and Liberty loyalty in his heart. He and I were the only two in the parking lot later cleaning off cars and sliding home.... and the next two days were not any better. Lights went out, customers had to come in four-wheel drives and the phones were off the hook, but we were there when they called and when they came, hot coffee in hand.... and a fresh hot doughnut... think those customers will be back? As they say in Alaska, " You betcha."

Small Gesture – Huge Impact

Dan Williams/Manager - Long Beach, CA

One of my first clients came to the office in early January. He supports his sister and her two children. He was eligible to claim the children on his tax return. We filed the return on a Friday. Three weeks later, the client came in to check on his refund. This time his head and face was bandaged up and he was walking with a cane. We called the IRS to check on his refund and found out they were auditing him. The client stated that he was shot in the face with a shotgun while being carjacked the night he filed his taxes. He desperately needed his tax return money, as he had not been able to work. We explained to the client what information he needed to provide to get the refund money sent. We helped him fax all the necessary paperwork to the IRS the same day.

Several weeks went by and the client's financial situation got worse. We continued to follow-up with the IRS. About eight weeks after filing the return, we printed a check. The client lived about two blocks from the office, so I put on my Lady Liberty costume, walked to his house, and presented the check. The client instantly started crying and the sister jumped up and gave me a hug. They thanked me multiple times and stated how much they appreciated my help. That small gesture of taking them their check made a huge impact in their lives.

We Have the Check for that Sweet Family Already!

By Nicole Bellenfant/Zee - Knoxville, TN

She came in flustered. She exclaimed that she needed a loan and that our competitor, whom she had been going to for ten years, no longer carried that product. She continued to explain that after an hour and a half interview with the other tax company, it was revealed they would not be able to offer a Refund Anticipation Loan. She revealed that her son had cancer and with all the medical bills they had, they were going to lose their house if they did not receive some money by Friday. She continued to explain that her son and husband were in the car waiting, and her husband was very aggravated. I explained to her we could help them, while I could not guarantee they would qualify for the loan, but we would do all we could to help their family.

My dear sweet mother, who is my office manager, has spent her entire life as a volunteer, working with terminally ill children. I had spent the previous 12 years as a fundraiser for non-profits prior to being a Liberty Franchisee. Mom immediately began gathering up giveaways around the office to give to the child. She filled a bag with t-shirts, crayons, flashlights and candy. The couple came in and it was obvious the husband was upset. My mother and I sat and played with their son, while the couple started their return. Her husband asked several times if we could be certain they would get their money fast and, unfortunately, we could not. They had to qualify for the loan and that is a process we have no control over. As they worked on their return, I leaned over the desk and said in a soft voice, so not to embarrass them, "we realize you've had a tough year and it would be my pleasure to prepare your taxes for free this year." They looked at me with blank expressions and nodded. I was a little taken aback because I did expect a thank you, but I know stress can cause you to be unresponsive at times.

The couple finished their return and left, anxiously clutching their giveaways, paperwork, and child. We practically followed them to their car, thanking them for coming in and promising to call as soon as we heard about their loan. Thanks to John Hewitt's reputation and relationship with the IRS, that year, not only did we have a loan product but also we were testing a program with the IRS called MEF that enabled returns to be acknowledged faster. This also meant loans could be issued faster. We of course did not tell the family that, as we didn't want to get their hopes up.

An hour later, my mother burst into tears at the processing computer. I ran to see what was wrong and she yelled, "WE HAVE THE CHECK ALREADY FOR THAT SWEET FAMILY!" We immediately picked up the phone and through our tears told them to come get their check! They were not losing their house!

She came running in almost as frazzled as the first time. She asked if we were certain it was theirs. We held out the check and she clutched it and started to cry. She thanked us profusely. She also apologized. She said the reason they had not reacted when I first offered to do their return was that they were worried that I was trying to trick them. She said it had been so long since anyone had shown any compassion to their situation, that it must be a lie to get them to leave our competitor, who told them no one had a loan anymore. She hugged us and we all cried. Even her stoic husband shed tears as he gave us his heartfelt gratitude. We prayed with her for her child and family and she left. I don't believe there was a dry eye in the office when she left.

The hard part about only seeing your clients once or twice a year is that you miss them when its not tax time. This is especially the case with this family. My mom always tells our clients when they leave our office, "You are our family now. We have a family reunion once a year at this time, and I hope you will join us again next year!" This could not be truer with this family. There are always hugs and stories when they come in. Jared calls my mom "Mamaw" and he brings her pictures from school as he is growing up and is now a very healthy young boy. For the past four years, they have been one of our best customers, referring everyone they know, telling them we saved their house, but more importantly that we cared about them when no one else did.

At this past season's reunion we were saddened to hear that the mother was having some health issues that had put more burden on their family. When we explained that we would like to do their return for free because they were receiving less of a refund then they originally thought, she explained she would like to still pay us to receive the $50 cash we offer customers. I whispered to my preparer to go ahead and do the return for free and still give them the $50 cash. She cried once again and smiled at her husband and exclaimed, "Now we can get groceries." My employee asked me why I went ahead and gave them the $50 when they weren't able to pay. I explained that we were family, and that it was the right thing to do and the way of Liberty. I can't put a number on what their friendship means to me, and that it is an honor to have them as clients and to serve them.

One of Our Proudest Moments

Johnathan King/Zee - Frisco, TX

This past tax season, a couple walked in our office and they were drenched in sweat. We had already done their taxes and they were just waiting for their refund, in which case I knew something was wrong because I had spoken with the wife just the day before.

I was with a customer and then wrapped that return up, and greeted them and introduced myself to the two kids, ages 5 and 6, who I hadn't met previously. I went through our normal routine and offered them chips and soda and then asked what was wrong? They asked to use the phone because their van had broken down and they just walked 3 miles carrying both the kids. They felt embarrassed but had to stop and get something to drink at our office.

What I learned from this point were the horrible series of events that occurred in the last 48 hours. The kids were the husband's children from a prior relationship. Their mother's apartment had burned down a few days before and they were displaced and our clients had to go and pick them up. The children were telling stories of the fire and all the smoke (it was sad and cute at the same time) and they were letting us know how far they had to walk, and how their toys got "burnt up" in the fire.

At this point there was little we could do but, luckily, I had the big Liberty Tax wrapped Hummer and asked if they would like a ride. It was the least I could do. I loaded the kids up with snacks and sodas and brought the family to their small home, which they were sharing with a handful of other family members.

Thankfully, their direct deposit posted the next day and I received a call at the office thanking us for everything we had done. I'll never forget that because it was definitely one of our proudest moments this season.

Restoring Faith in Good Human Beings

By Randolph Brooks/Tax Preparer - Columbia, SC

After finishing the opening checklist for the store early, I opened at 8:50 am. Almost immediately, an elderly lady came in and told me that she needed to get her taxes done. Talking with her, I discovered that her husband had died in the middle of 2013. She claimed that her daughter had been trying to take what little money she had left and had been stealing her mail. As she talked, she kept a very tight grip on her late husband's death certificate. I expressed my condolences and promised to help her in any way that I could. It was obvious that the lady was very senile, coupled with being very distraught over her situation as she awaited the probate process to clear.

She brought in a 1099-R pension statement, but it was for the year 2010, no W-2s, and no Social Security statements for herself or her late husband. I went online and found the phone numbers for the pension company and for the Social Security Administration and wrote it all down for the lady on a separate piece of paper for her future reference. I called the pension company and was able to explain the situation to a customer representative. I handed the phone over to the lady and then helped her with the discussion. The customer representative confirmed the pension numbers for me to use (which had not changed from the 2010 statement) and promised to send a duplicate 1099-R.

I then showed the lady what a Social Security statement looked like and she told me that she thought that she remembered seeing the two documents. Rather than call the Social Security office, I let her go home to find the documents. She returned very elated with the two statements and I was able to enter all the data. She realized small federal and state refunds, but the fees would have taken all of the refunds and forced her to pay some money. With permission from my supervisor, I gave her a free return, which I felt was the right thing to do.

Since her husband was deceased, I had to do a paper return to include a copy of the death certificate and include a Form 1310 "Statement of Person Claiming Refund Due a Deceased Taxpayer." Everything had to be printed to wet-sign. I then put the returns in envelopes with stamps and told the lady that I would get them in the mail. It took a lot of time but it was worth it.

She wanted to know how much she owed Liberty Tax Service. I told her not to worry about it. I was glad to help her. I could see that she was overjoyed and almost in tears. After the experience with her daughter, the sweet lady told me that I had restored her faith in good human beings---and that she would be back next year with Liberty Tax Service!!

The Tenaciousness of the Liberty Tax Team
By Shannon Bird/General Manager - Yakima, WA

Early in February, a family came to us to file four years worth of tax returns. They were quiet, friendly and humble, and quickly had everyone in the office smiling. They weren't sure they were even going to get a refund thanks, in part, to prior difficulties with an ex-spouse and the IRS. But they were trying to get into a home and needed to file all the back tax returns. Excitedly, the preparer told them they had refunds coming – enough to get them in the home! This was their chance that something good was finally going to happen to them! Because they couldn't afford to pay, the fees from the returns were to be taken out of their 2013 tax refund. They opted for a debit card to receive their refunds. We gave them a good deal and they left very happy knowing Liberty Tax had done a great job in preparing their tax returns and ensuring they would receive all the refunds available to them.

Then, something strange happened. On Feb. 15th, they called to check the status of their refund and our records indicated their card should have been funded four days earlier. But the card balance still showed zero and we hadn't been notified of the card funding. So where was the money? We contacted the card company who verified the card numbers, then told us to call the IRS because they showed the card had been activated and funded. The customer called the card company as well, only to be told to wait patiently. We contacted Liberty Corporate and asked for their help.

After four days with no answers, the customer was getting more and more desperate but, amazingly, remained calm and courteous to all the Liberty staff. You see, they were waiting on this $7000 refund to get into a new home, and hoping they didn't lose the home to someone else. They had already given their notice to their landlord and packed up all their meager belongings. Both parents were between jobs, and their three teenage children were trying to continue in school, depending on their parents to figure it all out. The prior landlord couldn't allow them to stay since he had rented the property. These people were just down on their luck, had no home to go to, no resources for funds. Our hearts were breaking for this nice family and we didn't know where to turn or how to help as the response kept coming back, "We're researching it." They still had the card, which should have had thousands of dollars on it, but not a single cent had been put on it. And to make matters worse, with nowhere else to turn, the family had to move into a relative's single-car garage. Can you imagine – two adults and three teenagers in high school living in a single-car garage?

We wrote emails, made phone calls, nothing was getting us answers. Finally, in desperation, we even went so far as to email John Hewitt himself. On Feb. 21st, six days after we began this refund-seeking journey, I spoke with a Net-Spend manager by the name of Kevin. He vowed to track down the funds even though his records showed the problem lay elsewhere than with the bank. Meanwhile, unbelievably, these customers continued to refer their friends to Liberty Tax, never once uttering a negative word against us! They stopped by to check on the status and we gave them coupons for free hamburgers, tacos, coffees and haircuts. Several departments at Liberty Corporate also leapt into action that day – the team was relentless and amazing! We were headed into the weekend with no faith in hearing anything until Monday, Feb. 24th, but on Saturday, Feb. 22nd at 2:36 PM, we got a call from our Area Developer and Support, Geoff Knapp. The card had been loaded!

As soon as I got off the phone, I called the customer. Darn, just his voicemail! I left a message to please call. At 4 PM, the client called back. He sounded so dejected, so beat up by life. My heart just swelled. I had one of the greatest pleasures of my career with Liberty in telling him the card was funded – they now had their money, they now had options. There was a long pause and I finally said, "Robert? Say something, please." With a quiver in his voice, he quietly said, "Thank you, thank you so much. We just left the pawnshop. We were going to pawn our last valuables because we need food."

The happy ending? They moved out of the relative's garage and into the home they called their dream home, thanks to the tenaciousness of the Liberty Tax team.

A Customer for Life

By Connie Moore/Zee, CPA - Baltimore, MD

It was a very cold February night when a new customer walked in the door with his girlfriend. He had been unemployed for many months and just started a new job. The $50 Cash in a Flash brought him in the door. When I met with him and completed the return, the refund was very small and not enough to even cover the preparation fees. Since he just started a job and seemed fairly desperate, I told him that I would do the return for free. He was upset and said he needed the $50 to buy oil for heating a room in his home that night. I then said that as a Christian I want to help so here is $50, and I will still do the return for free. He was so happy that he and his girlfriend shed some tears. He told me he would give me back the $50, but I told him that was not necessary. About a month later, he came in and asked for me and only me. He handed me the $50 and thanked me for the kindness and said I had a customer for life.

FROM OUR

RAVING FANS

FROM OUR RAVING FANS

Liberty ROCKS!

By Debra Bubash/Customer post on Fanaticalatliberty.com

This tax season was stressful enough, and I was wondering how I was going to afford to get my taxes done this year because I was not financially able to go to H&R Block or any other tax accountant. The past two years, I tried my hand at it with Turbo Tax, and I believe I possibly sold myself short and did not receive the most of my return that was available to me.

I stressed over this immensely, until a friend told me about Liberty Tax Service. I was told that every year Liberty Tax Service provides a promotional service that covers the cost for Health Care employees to have their taxes done at no cost. I wasn't sure if I should believe that this would be such a great experience, being that there would be no cost. However, I gave Liberty Tax Service a try and to my surprise I was more pleased with this experience than I can remember having in a very long time.

The employees at Liberty Tax Service were so friendly and kind. They accommodated me and made me feel like I was the most important person they ever served. They thanked me for my service in the Health Care field and treated me like I was a special guest. I really appreciated that they thanked me for my service in health care. Also, I was waited on the moment I walked through the door. Every employee acknowledged me and smiled and offered me coffee or any beverage to my liking. They answered every question I had and asked me questions to complete my taxes to the best of their ability. They were thorough and prompt and completed my taxes in a very timely manner. Also, they gave me coupons for my friends to have their taxes done, too. So, if my friends are willing to try their services, I would receive monetary recognition for that, as well.

I was so very pleased and satisfied with the service that the employees gave to me at Liberty Tax Service; it is all I have talked about for two weeks. I will return next year and I will highly recommend Liberty Tax Service to everyone I know that is looking for a wonderful and pleasant experience when facing tax season. It is so refreshing to know that there is still excellent service available in a world that doesn't seem to care anymore about

Customer Service. Thank You Liberty Tax Service! YOU ROCK! Sincerely, Debra Bubash :)

They Genuinely Care About Us

Mechille Burke/Customer - Knoxville, TN

Since 1985, we had been going to the same big name tax company. My sister worked there and we didn't think much about it. We just went in every year like clockwork. That all changed in 2010.

That year, my family went to do our taxes at our usual tax company. The whole ordeal took us around an hour and a half, and at the end we were told they could not offer us a refund anticipation loan. We had always received the loan and this couldn't be a worse year not to get it. My 7-year-old son, Jared, had been battling a very rare and deadly form of cancer and he was very sick. We were leaving in 9 days to go to St. Jude's Children's Research Hospital. We were relying on the loan of our income tax to help make our expenses to get there and our mortgage was due that weekend, as well. Not only did this tax business tell us they couldn't give us a loan but they insisted that no other tax company would be able to offer a loan that year either.

Luckily, we passed a Liberty Tax Service office on the way. They had an employee outside dressed like the Statue of Liberty who smiled and waved as we passed. It now seemed like a beacon of hope and I suggested we go back and see what they could do.

I walked into the office, leaving Jared and Billy in the car to scope it out. Judy welcomed me with a big smile. I inquired about the refund anticipation loan and Judy said yes, they did have one. I anxiously asked her if she was sure. She said yes, she was sure and she asked if I was ok? She said I seemed worried. I explained our situation and Judy put her arm around me and said why don't you go get your family and let us try to help you.

As we walked in Nicole, the owner introduced herself and her mother, Judy. We were ushered to a seat and offered beverages and food. Our preparer smiled and started sorting our paperwork, while Nicole and Judy took Jared to the toy area and gave him t-shirts and crayons and other fun things. During our interview, Nicole explained that she would like to prepare our taxes for free this year because we had such a hard year. We weren't sure if they could really get us a tax loan or if our taxes would really be free, but they seemed nice and we figured we didn't have anything to lose. But, I have to admit I was skeptical, as was my husband. However, everything seemed to be in order and these people were some of the nicest people I had ever met. Before leaving, Judy and Nicole gave us a hug and told us they would be praying with us for a check to come soon and for the health of Jared.

We got home and our phone rang. It was Judy. She said they had a check for us. I couldn't believe it. We had just left their office. It seemed like a trick or a mistake. We got back in the car and drove back. Lo and behold, they did have a check for us! We expected to hear from them in two or three days and here it was less than an hour later. Judy and Nicole were crying with me as I clutched that check, so thankful that the Lord had provided again for my family. I told them that it had been so long since anyone had shown compassion to my family; I wasn't sure how to take them on our first visit. After all, things that seem too good to be true usually aren't true. My husband is a very hard working stoic man. We don't like to ask for favors and we've always made it, no matter what life has thrown at us. As he tried to express his gratitude, I was surprised when a big tear ran down his face. Judy assured us we didn't need to thank them as she put her arm around our shoulders. She said life had been unfair to our family and with tears in her eyes she told us they were honored to be able to help us. We cried and hugged and I promised we would be back and I would tell everyone to come to their office.

I was excited the next year to go visit them. I wasn't sure if they would remember us, after all it had been a year since we had seen them. As soon as I walked in, Judy exclaimed our names and ran over to hug us. Every year since, we walk into that office and are greeted with smiles, hugs, and happiness. We always have a little reunion where we catch each other up on our lives before we start our taxes. Jared calls Judy "Mamaw" and he can't wait to see her every year. It really feels like family whenever we visit or call. I used to hate doing my taxes, but since 2010, I can't wait to spend some time with my newfound family.

This year, I've had extreme health issues haunt me. It seems like Jared and I trade turns all the time with our ups and downs. When I went to visit this year, Nicole, upon hearing of my illness and many hospitalizations, told the preparer not to charge us this year. My husband works so hard and we've always been able to pay all our bills one way or another. I told her we wanted to pay, but she insisted. She winked and told us it was the family discount and next year when we were all healthier we could pay again. We aren't the kind of family that asks for anything from anyone. We've never asked for anything at Liberty Tax, but we've never had to. Nicole and Judy have seen our need and responded. They care about us. They genuinely care about us. You can't find that kind of care today anymore, or so I thought before walking into that Liberty tax office.

I've learned that sometimes things that seem too good to be true are even better than they first appear. In Liberty Tax Service not only have we found excellent tax preparers and customer service, but we've gained a family that cares about my family beyond the numbers on a 1040 or an invoice, but in our lives. Why would I ever want to go anywhere else?

Jeweled Eagle: God Bless America

Joy Lynn McCavit/ Customer - Wasilla, AK

After I decided my life-long dream of becoming a professional artist was a real possibility - even though I wasn't sure how to begin walking out that dream - I was willing and decided to take whatever steps necessary to begin painting, while caring for my son. He wound up needing to be cared for full-time and home schooled, as well. This step meant having to quit my career with the State of Alaska.

Even though caring for my son was very hard and the sacrifice of possibly eating through my retirement, long before it was time, was a real concern, I had to think of my son's needs first. My quitting to be with him kept him from ever requiring long term respite care again, except for once which also gave me the last really deep hands-on training that I desperately needed. It built confidence as well as understanding for exactly what was needed to help him function and thrive as he grew up.

I walked into Liberty Tax prior to April 15th, feeling defeated because of what I thought we would owe the IRS after everything else that we had already paid out of pocket that year for medical treatment and care; we had given up so much to care for our son. Not only were they wonderful and professional in our local office, but I couldn't imagine going anywhere else because of their loving, hometown touch. This particular year, because of our son's Aspergers diagnosis on top of a couple of other diagnoses, we had a pleasant surprise awaiting us with just the right people gathering together at exactly the right time. The money we had spent on medical expenses and costs for all of the extra care and counseling, and because of having to give up employment and retirement, well, that sacrifice for exactly our circumstances was cause for a small refund.

Our lady who worked with us that day had family who dealt with issues like our son. Because of her personal knowledge of the care needed, she did some checking and a week later we had good news. We qualified for a special filing that would recoup enough to pay for the last entire respite stay out of state. It was a blessing that she was exactly the right person to help us. I feel like these small, hometown Liberty offices are amazing because they go the extra mile with a huge friendly smile, every single time you enter their doors.

After that, our family quickly continued to heal and I did get to step into my dream job. I am now a full-time professional artist and work with a couple of non-profits, locally, sharing what I love the most - to bring blessings to my entire community. There is a picture on my Facebook page with one of my newest paintings that was; by the way, definitely inspired in the beginning by Liberty Tax and the patriotism I see decorating all of the offices. I titled it: Jeweled Eagle: God Bless America." The freedom and blessings I see in my life from the little things like paying your taxes in a franchise that is as wonderful as Liberty Tax - for that I would like to say: "Thank you!"

Without the Stress

By Lisa Ekstrom/Customer - Kentland, IN

Teaching-stress. Not enough hours in the day. Too much paperwork as a special education teacher. Spring break was right around the corner and I still had my taxes to do over break. *Big sigh.*

I have a friend who has a Liberty franchise in Richmond, Indiana, who I met while volunteering with Blue Stars Drum and Bugle Corps, where our sons march together. Last year, I had mentioned "I'll let you do my taxes next year," … and nothing more was said. One week ago, I posted my frustration on Facebook about having to spend time completing my taxes, as well as that of my daughter. Soon, I saw a FB message, "Hey! I thought I was doing your taxes this year." That was all it took.

We texted, e-mailed, and did a FaceTime chat, and all the paperwork I had organized for myself was boxed off and sent by certified mail for Liberty of Richmond to complete for me. I got a text that it would be started this week.... just a few days after it was received. I cannot tell you the relief and sheer joy this brought to my face. I knew that my documents were in good hands and that the taxes would be completed correctly and efficiently. There is no better feeling... other than knowing I had the week to myself without the stress of doing the tax work. Thank you, Liberty and Diana!!

NOBODY ELSE Will Do Our Taxes!

Melissa Hylton/New Customer - Christiansburg, VA

I went in to the Christiansburg, Virginia store and Ms. Angela Woolwine did our taxes. WOW! From the get-go, she offered us coffee. She was extremely friendly the entire time, chatted with us during, and even gave us a discount.

She did a SUPER job, and got us the maximum refund she could. She wasn't a bit worried about anything else in the world other than doing our taxes and, to me, that is SO IMPORTANT!!!! I can tell you this; NOBODY ELSE will be doing our taxes from now on. Y'all hang on to that young lady. She's OUTSTANDING!

(From Fanaticalatliberty.com blog: Tell us about yourself?)

Just your average Mom. I stay at home, and work hard at taking care of my children and my husband. Before doing this, though, I worked many years doing customer service myself, so I know good customer service when I see it!

Fighter

Tammy Jueneman/Customer - Casper, WY

Good afternoon! My experience with Liberty Tax Service actually began 30 years ago. Your tax preparer, Teresa Seiver, has been my best friend for that many years. The last year has been a roller coaster, to say the least.

In February of 2013, I was forced to sell my business and get back to a regular job that supplied me with benefits to support my teenage son. That's ok, because I will do anything to take care of him. I was fortunate enough to go to work for a company that is very caring and compassionate. In October of 2013, I was diagnosed with Stage 4 Metastatic Breast Cancer. For the last 6 months, we have been doing chemotherapy and the first of March, I had surgery. Now we will deal with radiation.

With the sale of my business (mostly CFD – Contract for Differences), I have been so worried what would happen with my taxes. My previous CPA didn't seem to want to really go the extra mile when doing my taxes. I never got a refund and was always charged a very large amount for preparation. I just knew that the IRS was going to take everything I had. Thanks to Teresa, and the rest of the staff at your store (in Casper), I'm actually getting a refund! It was like the weight of the world was lifted off my shoulders. With the refund I'm getting, I was able to purchase a much-needed new bed. That new bed makes my life so much easier, getting up and down.

When I stopped in at Liberty Tax Service to pick up my finished taxes, the franchise owner, Sandy Sowder, handed me a personal card from her… It said "Congratulations on being a Survivor." I'm not done with my fight yet, but with support from people like Sandy and Teresa, I will win this battle. Thank you for reading my story and for helping me with my taxes. I will go to Liberty Tax Service from now on!

Amazing Service!

Barbara Hart/Customer - Virginia Beach, VA

I was trying to help my 57-year-old cousin find health insurance at the end of March, so that he could avoid the penalty for failing to have health insurance. I found online that Liberty was a site that could help him sign up.

While he works as a self-employed upholsterer, his income is modest. He has multiple health problems including diabetes, seizure disorder, dental ailments, attention deficit disorder, and learning disabilities. This is not a person who has an e-mail address, access to the Internet, much disposable income or options for health insurance, given multiple pre-existing conditions. I made an appointment for him and accompanied him.

We visited the Liberty Tax, Ferrell Parkway office in Virginia Beach. He received amazing service from Susanna Muller. It was time-consuming and complicated. She was extraordinarily patient and helpful in the two hours it took to sort through his situation. He was helped in analyzing what kind of insurance he needed, advised of options, signed up for an email address, and counseled on income tax issues. This is an incredible community service for which my cousin is grateful. He and many others, I am sure, may actually get health care help through Liberty.

Many thanks to you, Susanna Muller, and Liberty Tax, Ferrell Parkway!!

Saved Thousands of Dollars

Robert Kihne/Customer - Saint Cloud, MN

My wife and I were going to do our own taxes this year, but changed our mind and went back to Liberty again this year. They literally saved me thousands of dollars. Liberty is My New Best Friend.

Fast and Easy to Understand

William Johnson/Customer - Sauk Rapids, MN

I have always had bad luck with taxes and tax preparation. People have made mistakes doing my taxes, costing me money. Things were a huge pain, especially with me being disabled.

My wife and I decided to try Liberty Tax Service after a really huge screw up by someone. We figured it wouldn't hurt... maybe even our luck might change. We came in that first time and it was fast and easy to understand. They fixed the problem. Because of this we have always come back to Liberty, and we are always trying to turn people towards them.

First Time Taxpayer

Micaella Gonzalez/Customer - Chicago, IL

I started working with UPS at 18. It was my first job right after graduating high school. Then a year goes by and all of sudden I get my W-2s and, of course, I didn't know what to do because I never had a job before. I then made an appointment with Liberty Tax and they were helpful, from talking on the phone to meeting in person.

They helped and talked me through everything, so I knew what was going on as a first time taxpayer. The employee gave me no problems and took the time to make sure I was signing and understanding the procedures for the processing. I was glad the experience went so well that I will continue going to Liberty Tax for help with my taxes.

Fantastic and Very Friendly

By Andrew Porteous/Customer - Northridge, CA

Last year, I tried to file my taxes myself. The process was painful and confusing and I somehow ended up paying more taxes. This year, I let the team at Liberty file my taxes. Not only was the process painless, but it was very easy and took less time than I imagined. What's more, I received money back this year!

The team at Liberty was fantastic and very friendly. I cannot fault them one little bit and I will definitely be returning to them next year.

Mom Didn't Raise No Fool

Tom Weidenhoefer/Customer - Orland Park, IL

Just before retirement, I accidentally found an offer from Liberty Tax to do my taxes for free. That's right, FREE. Well mom didn't raise no fool so I decided to give them a try. The franchise I went to was a newer franchise that was a very friendly/family -type operation and I was welcomed, as if I were part of the family.

The first year, as advertised, was free. The next few years I did pay for mine, but my daughter's forms were still free, or as you would say, on the house. Since the first year, not only have I returned each year, but have made two new friends and a new golfing buddy. Larry has now opened two other locations and is one of the hardest workers that you could ever meet.

I Trust Them

Mary Spinelli/Customer - Fort Collins, CO

Well, I used to have an accountant who worked for a big firm. He used to do my parent's taxes, so I trusted him and really thought he had my best interests in mind. The last year he did my taxes, he charged me almost $400.00 and I was stunned. My taxes were not complicated - the only change, I was newly divorced. No personal care or concern. Well, I couldn't afford to go back there.

My fiancé suggested Liberty Tax Service. It was close to where we lived and convenient. I walked in and ended up with an accountant (John Lopez) who helped me tremendously. He changed the way I had been filing (making me Head of Household) and ended up getting me money back from the previous two years.

He cared and spent time with me. He treated me like a family member. It was not what I was expecting with this business. I was thinking I would be just a number. The entire staff was professional and very kind. I will always go to Liberty Tax Service to get my taxes done. I trust them.

User Friendly Website

Joyce Wright/Customer - Macon, GA

Liberty Tax has a very user-friendly website, filled with lots of useful information. I have used them to do my return and this was one of the best experiences I have had with any tax service.

My tax preparer relocated and I felt lost, but I am going there again because no other service has been as efficient, fast and friendly as Liberty. The one thing I really love is that they provide support all year long.

Making Tax Season Less Stressful!

By Mariana Vandivier/Customer - Naples, FL

Second year in a row having my taxes prepared by Mr. Miles Ianacone at Liberty Tax. Miles exhibits the highest level of integrity and professionalism, exceeding my expectations.

I've had my taxes prepared by H&R Block for many years, and often left feeling unsatisfied, but being a creature of habit, I kept returning. Decided last year to give Liberty Tax a try and I'm happy I did. I have shared with many my high level of satisfaction and have encouraged them to give Liberty Tax and Miles a chance.

Thank you to both Liberty Tax and Miles Ianacone for making tax season less stressful!

Life, Liberty, and the Pursuit of Happiness

By Randel Jones-Carpenter/Customer - Westfield, MA

The whole uplifting experience begins with the team of wavers. Their friendly waves and smiles, teamed with their brilliant costumes, almost carry you into another world and away from one that can seem cold and distant at times. The dazzling performance is far from over though.

Upon entering a Liberty Tax office, it almost feels like home away from home with its seating area conducive to conversation, its coloring books and small knick-knacks for children, and its splendid array of choices for coffee, teas, chocolates, and other goodies. When the moment arises for you to be serviced, you are greeted as if a guest in their home and provided with an accurate and speedy service that I would imagine is unparalleled in the industry.

I salute Liberty Tax for their professionalism and willingness to reach out to people from all walks of LIFE, for their honoring our Lady Statue of LIBERTY as evidenced by the costumes of the wavers, and for their overall teamwork and creation of an atmosphere so consistent with HAPPINESS. They have truly honored the values set forth in our Declaration, namely Life, Liberty, and the Pursuit of Happiness. Thank you, Liberty Tax.

Wonderful Service

Norma P. Skeath/Customer - Naples, FL

My Liberty Tax story goes back several years now. I was posted in Guyana (the former British Guiana) between 2008 and 2012. Fortunately, I used to visit Southwest Florida during that time (I had previously lived there). I discovered Liberty Tax and, most importantly, I discovered Miles Ianacone in the Naples office.

Miles handled everything for me in the most efficient, speedy and nicest way possible. In 2012, I was transferred to Sri Lanka. Miles, again, has come to my rescue and we are able to do everything online. I greatly appreciate Liberty and, especially, Miles for this wonderful service.

Setting the Standard

Andrea Sullivan/ Customer - Casper, WY

I first met Sandy from Liberty Tax in Casper, Wyoming when I needed my taxes done, after I purchased my first house. I'd had my taxes done at H&R Block and Jackson Hewitt before but never had a sense that I was anything more than just a customer and, therefore, never felt a strong connection to either facility. I am a veteran and was able to utilize my VA Loan benefits for the first time and needed someone to help me file my taxes! I first went to H&R Block. Then to Jackson Hewitt. Neither facility had any information on how to handle my VA closing fees.

I was referred to Sandy after completely rejecting the idea that I knew how to file them! My first conversation with Sandy let me know that I was at the right place. Immediately, she knew the answer. Off the top of her head, she could tell me the current legislation and pending legislation that might affect me in the future. And that has been the standard that Sandy has set for herself and her employees. Again, when I became a volunteer with the dog rescue, the first person I called was Sandy. From her commitment to continuing education, she could guide me as to what I and other volunteers could claim and how to set about doing it. I referred my boyfriend who is a firefighter. She not only did his taxes, she educated him as to the exemptions he may be eligible for. This is how my life events go now, as I make a change, I then call Liberty Tax! This standard of knowledge in the field is upheld by all of her employees and I know that I am more than a customer there.

If it weren't enough that you are treated with respect, with a friendly disposition, and as a valued customer, Liberty Tax in Casper, Wyoming has also made a strong effort to reach out to the community, holding and participating in events for local charities. In fact, the dog rescue that I also volunteer with received an email from Mal, a Liberty Tax employee, offering to hold an event on our behalf! As a volunteer myself, and a veteran, I truly value this sense of community and passion to help others in all of the employees there and they will forever have my respect, as well as the respect of all of my friends that I have referred. I follow Liberty Tax on Facebook as well, because part of their reaching out to the community is to share articles that will be educational to taxpayers who aren't knowledgeable about tax preparation.

For these reasons (and more) I will always use Liberty Tax in Casper, Wyoming and am very proud of doing business at an establishment that is so dedicated to education in their field, the community, and their customers.

We Were Able to Have our Honeymoon

April Cook/Customer - Richmond, IN

Liberty Tax was the nicest best place we had ever been! My husband and I had been together for going on 8 years this year. Fighting all the odds, we have had a successful and wonderful marriage, but are too poor to have been able to have a honeymoon and spent our "honeymoon" at home, like any other day.

So thanks to Liberty Tax for getting us money back, we were able to have our honeymoon, FINALLY.

How Liberty Tax Changed Our Lives

By Donna and Paul Dufour/Customers - Enfield, CT

We have been using Liberty Tax for about five years now. Over the years, there have been a few changes in our income, and Liberty Tax has helped us file our taxes efficiently, as always, but two and a half years ago everything changed.

My husband, Paul, suffered a brain aneurysm and stroke, which left him disabled and a long recovery ahead of him. From the beginning, Liberty Tax has guided us, not only just at tax time, but also gave us important information about gathering medical and financial documents to prepare us for the next upcoming tax season. Skip Anderson, our main Liberty Tax man, was so patient and understanding - always polite and willing to go beyond for us, not just treating us like clients, but as real people. We always felt comfortable and knew we were in professional hands with this company.

Skip and his team have always done their best in advising us with our taxes, college deductions, and medical documents over the last two years. He even helped us with our IRA deductions (used for medical bills) so we would not get penalized. It would make my head spin if we were ever trying to think of doing our taxes ourselves, or with any other service. No matter how many times we have called them (and we called them A LOT), Liberty Tax people were always patient and understanding with us to go over our taxes and finding a better way to save us money.

We've had to deal with many hospitals, doctors, and insurance companies that left us feeling confused, frustrated, and treated us like a number. I can't tell you how much we appreciate the kindness and professionalism from the people at Liberty Tax. It's nice to know there are people out there who really care about the people they serve.

Creature of Habit

Ginger Dureya/Customer - New Braunfels, TX

I will start by saying I am a creature of habit. Every year, for 7 years, I got my taxes done at the same place. I liked them - they were fast and nice and I got to know them.

When my husband and I got married and moved to New Braunfels, tax season rolled around and we decided it was just too far to go to the old place. So we did a little research and decided on Liberty Tax. Now as a reminder, I am a creature of habit so I wasn't so sure, but when we walked in we were met with  smiling faces. The lady that helped us (and I am sad to say that I cannot remember her name) was so incredibly nice! I told her that it was our first time there and I hoped that I brought everything I needed. She made the process so easy. We talked and laughed about our kids and pets. Even after we signed the papers, we stayed for another 15 minutes chit-chatting.

People sometimes roll their eyes when I tell them that is why we are happy with you guys but, hey, 5 years later and you still make us feel just as comfortable as when we first walked in!

Keep up the Good Work!

Shalonda Stewart/Customer - Fridley, MN

Hi, my name is Shalonda Stewart and I'm a mother of six and I love Liberty Tax. I've been a customer since 2004 - I love the employees and the business is great. I've never had any problems, always been accurate. I haven't filed with anyone since I started with Liberty Tax. I love you guys - keep up the good work!!!!!

Liberty Tax Really Gets All Your Money Back

Quiateesha Jones/Customer - Albany, GA

The very first time filing my taxes I was working at Burger King and didn't at all think I would receive much back in taxes. My mom told me about Liberty Tax in Albany, Georgia. I went with her and applied one day before going to work. The manager of the store sat down and helped me start filing, she informed me of every single thing she did, she showed me the screen as she went, I wasn't blind to anything.

I received about $1700 and I saved every penny and purchased my first car. I am still thankful to this day. The lady helped me because, doing it myself, I would have been lost. I appreciated everything Liberty Tax has done for me because, technically, I wouldn't have my car and my car was something I desperately needed, knowing I had a one-year old to take back and forth to the babysitter, when I had work and school.

This year I filed with Liberty Tax, as well, and also had four former H&R Block filers to file with Liberty Tax. This year, I received enough to pay off outstanding bills, gas up my car, and have spending as well as saving money. Other companies do advertise, saying they'll get all your money back, but Liberty Tax really gets all your money back and their fees aren't high at all.

Thank you so much Liberty Tax for ALL you've done for families, my friends, and me!

We are Eternally Grateful!

Scott & Faith White/Customer - Franklin, PA

I opened my new law practice last September and before that my wife did our taxes for years, due to the fact it was easy when I worked for a company! But this year, we decided we needed a professional to do them. So my wife knows the owner of the Liberty Tax in Franklin and Oil City, plus she ran a nice trailer court for many years, so we knew she'd be the best to go to, being she is also a business owner!!!

So when we went there we had an estimate of what we would get back. Well, she and her employees got us way more than we had anticipated, so we are eternally grateful to Jackie and her awesome employees!!! Plus, we will be using them to do our taxes quarterly! It was a great experience and they catered to our every need and even had a play area for kids!!

So when you get your taxes done, I highly recommend Liberty Tax to anyone!! It was a pleasure doing business with them and we will continue to do so every year!! Thank you all at Liberty Tax in Franklin, Pa!!!! :)

A Healthy Refund

By Mike Mamola/Customer - Arden, NC

We established our jewelry business in 2012, just a "mom and pop" operation. Like many people, we used Turbo Tax for years prior to setting up our business. Once we did, Turbo Tax just wasn't the way to go. I spent two days using Turbo Tax, most of that time pulling my hair out and was totally confused.

So we decided to visit Liberty's office on Airport Rd. in Arden, NC. A gentleman by the name of Clive Broadbent handled both our personal and business tax returns. Clive found us every possible deduction and then some, and we were quite happy to find out we'd be getting a sizeable refund. So, naturally, we made another visit to the same Liberty office this February.

Walking through the door, Clive spotted us immediately, remembered our names, and welcomed us back to Liberty. Once again, we received a healthy refund for tax year 2013. You can bet that, once again, we'll be paying Clive and friends a visit in early 2015. Thanks, Liberty!

More Than Just a Number

Mary Hoegsted/Tax Preparer - Union Grove, WI

During my unemployment phase in the year 2010, I re-established my tax preparer skills by attending a tax course with Liberty Tax Service in Burlington, WI. Upon completion of the course, I was able to feel reconnected to my customer service abilities within myself, and proceed to continue to this day providing customer service in my accounting field.

Liberty Tax Service gives top quality service to all customers and makes them feel that they are more than just a number in the scope of everyday life.

You Guys are Awesome!

Sterling Williams/Customer - Westfield, MA

Liberty Tax was an amazing help when tax season came around. It was my first year having to get my taxes done on my own. Unfortunately, I was having problems obtaining my W-2 forms from my employers and because one of my employers never sent me a W-2, I could not get my taxes done.

One day, I finally decided I would just go to the local Liberty Tax and see if they could help me. Upon arrival, a Liberty Tax employee acknowledged me right when I walked in, which I liked a lot. After a short wait, I was assisted. I explained my situation with my W-2s and immediately they knew what to do. She explained that I could possibly look up my last W-2 online. She went to a website on her computer and allowed me to use her phone to call Price Rite and find my employer store code and PIN. Then we looked up the W-2 online and she was able to finish my taxes.

I had a great experience on my first visit to Liberty Tax and I will happily be returning there next tax season and whenever I have questions. Thank You, Liberty Tax!! You guys are awesome!!

Qualified Tax Professionals

Rita Hurd/Customer - Elk River, MN

Our tax prep person retired after 20 years and we didn't know who to trust. We chose a family friend's daughter and while she worked very closely with us, she mistakenly missed several items.

Thankfully, Liz at Elk River, MN Liberty Tax checked into this when she did our taxes for 2013, finding us an additional $500.00. We learned to only have qualified tax professionals help us in the future.

Thank you, Liz at Liberty Tax!!

We Love Liberty!

Lindsay Bartlett/Customer - Chico, CA

We LOVE Liberty!!!! Had never used Liberty before; I filed taxes for our family using an online service in the past, and ended up with a bill from the IRS for items missed or entered incorrectly. I also feel like our taxes were pretty "messy" this year - we sold a house, moved to a new city, bought a house, made significant improvements to both homes, I am a Realtor, and worked two part time "side" jobs, and we have two kids in daycare. Whew!

Took our huge pile of "stuff" to Timothy late in the evening on a Friday night, spent only an hour in the office with him, (while our two young kids were entertained with movies, coloring, TV provided by Liberty in the office). AMAZING! Timothy related to us on a personal and professional level, helped us get our tax bill down by over $1000 from what I projected myself using one of the big name "online" filing companies.

The fee to prepare our taxes paled in comparison to the amount we saved - we are absolutely thankful and had a very pleasant experience. Timothy went the extra mile to help us realize deductions we hadn't considered, and was so pleasant to work with. Very happy to have found Liberty - we will certainly be using them again!! Thanks, so much.

Liberty Helped When I Needed Them Most

Shauntelle Johnson/Customer - Chicago, Illinois

Liberty Tax touched my life because, without them, I would have truly been lost this year without the funds provided to me through their services! I am so grateful, seeing that they came right on time when my mother passed away on Jan 30, 2014!

I wasn't going to file at first, because I didn't even get my W-2s until the day before. I was hardly thinking about doing taxes, seeing that the woman that meant the world to me was battling breast cancer! So February 5, 2014, I went ahead and filed and received $50 for filing and got my picture taken! Which I didn't want to do! But in the end, I'm glad I did because my little sister was still living with my mother at the time of her death and she needed help financially!! So I did what I thought my mom would have wanted me to do - I gave her the majority of my tax refund to help her out so she would be able to get back on her feet! Seeing that she just graduated prior to my mother's untimely death!

She was so excited to be able to leave Chicago, due to the violence here in this city! She is now back at E.I.U. and trying to pursue another degree! While I'm here still trying to maintain in this crazy city! Without Liberty Tax being so conveniently close to my mother's house at the time (since I was there during arrangements for her memorial) I would have probably never got around to doing them at all! But I knew my family needed me, especially my baby sister! I was so grateful for my refund even if I couldn't really use it for my son or myself!

Thanks again - Liberty really helped me when I needed them the most! :)

I Was in a Panic!

Meredith Vuylsteke, Customer - Hillsboro, OR

I had been working for the city for five years as a library clerk. I was elated when I was finally hired full time! At last! Insurance, full-time pay, all the perks of working full time! I was not smiling when I filed my first tax return by myself, though! I had always filed my own returns electronically. Well, I went to figure my taxes out and I about fell out of my chair! It said I owed both federal and state taxes! Not just a little, but a lot! Being a single mother, money is not flush, but we get by. I was used to getting about $3,400 back each year. I was not used to even thinking I had to pay! I was in a panic! So I loaded up all my paperwork and headed down to my local Liberty Tax office.

The woman there couldn't have been nicer! She sat down and we went over everything. It took her just a short time and she had my return all done and filed! I received a good-sized federal refund and only had to pay a small state tax. Yeeaah! I couldn't have been happier! Now, every year, I go down to the same office and have them do my taxes. I even got to see the "Changing of the Liberty" crew! One (waver) was just coming in as another went out. Funny stuff!

Liberty Turned My Day Around!

Nicole Rozman/New Customer - Pittsburgh, PA

I came in today upset because I found out from H&R Block that I was only receiving a few hundred dollars. I was told to come to Liberty to get a second opinion, and I'm very pleased that I did. H&R Block told me that my schooling didn't matter this year, however, it really did and instead of only getting $500, I'm receiving $1600.

I have to say this turned my day around 100% - and I will continue to come here every tax season. Thank you for all your help!!!!

Thank You for Helping Me

Anonymous/Customer - Baton Rouge, LA

A few years ago, I filed with my husband and because he owed back child support, they kept my money. So, for years I didn't file for fear they would keep my money. So thanks to y'all, I found out I could file without my husband on my taxes, and now I get my refund every year. Thank you for helping me.

I Will Never Use Another Tax Prep Company!

Ann Fost/Customer - Richmond, IN

Eric & Diana Bowman are simply the kindest people I could ever hope to have in my life. Last year presented many personal challenges for me, including a separation from my husband, a subsequent stay in an in-house treatment facility for my husband, two moves with my children, my husband losing his job, and our necessity to file for bankruptcy. We essentially walked away from our lives and comforts of 15 years to deal with my husband's addiction.

Our finances are a mess and somewhat disorganized from the moves. Richmond's Liberty staff was so very helpful and compassionate with me! Diana looked over every line of my return to make sure everything that could be done was done AFTER her staff prepared my return. Most tax prep places are a mill and would not take the time, but Diana did.

I will never use another tax prep company!

You Are My Liberty Tax Family

By Alisha McWhorter/Client - OH

I am at a loss of words when it comes to Liberty Tax. Liberty is not just another place to get your taxes done, but a group of people that become your family the second you walk through the door. I have the absolute enjoyment of going there for the past five years and every time I go, they are friendly and very fast. They take the time to get to know you. When you're there you are not just another customer, but a new friend. Liberty takes the time for you.

I have had the chance to work for Liberty for a short time and I absolutely loved it. When given the opportunity again, I will go back and work for you. I love that you give a tax class to people who want to learn more and prepare other people's taxes. All I can say is keep up the great work. I will forever be a returning customer because, to me, you are more than just Liberty Tax; you are my Liberty Tax family.

GIVE LOYALTY, GET LOYALTY

God, Family, and Business

By Dennis Dercks/Area Developer - WI

Liberty is a great business, but it is also a family. I remember at a convention a few years ago, when John Hewitt stated his three most important values:

1) God
2) Family
3) Business

Those values, and their order, resonated with me.

I have been an Area Developer since December of 2001 with Liberty Tax. It has been a wonderful 12 years of success and support. In December, 2012, that support was never more evident to me. That month, just before the tax season was to start, I suffered a serious injury. My wife contacted Pam Deitz, my Regional Director, to let her know of the accident and that I would be in physical therapy for several months, unable to support the Zees in our DMA. Liberty immediately reassured my family that we did not need to worry-- they would support our area and keep me in their prayers. Within a week, other Area Developers offered support, and sent cards and gifts for well wishes and healing. Ryan and Tiffany Dodson came from North Carolina to Wisconsin and personally met with our Zees, assured our Zees they would personally support them, and then continued to follow through on that support-- not only while the Dodsons were in Wisconsin, but also when they returned to North Carolina to handle their own busy tax season. Other members of the Liberty Team assisted our Zees as well, and helped my wife who was trying to straddle dealing with the crisis in our family and helping with the issues of the DMA.

While Liberty is on the path to be the top tax service by 2020, John and the rest of the Liberty family stay true to the professed top values of God, family, and business. When tragedy hit that forced me out of the Liberty loop (and life in general) at the most critical juncture of the year, Liberty truly treated me like family. The professed values I remember John stating at that convention did not ring hollow. They rang true. Perhaps that is why they resonated with me at the time of the convention, and they still do. It is certainly why my family and I continue to keep our Liberty Family in our prayers. God bless us all.

Liberty Gave My Heart a Chance to Heal

Nikki S. Montgomery/Project Manager - Liberty Corporate

Five years ago, I lived in Florida, and my son and I were homeless. I hadn't worked a steady job in about three years. One day, I was at a friend's house on their computer, and found an old friend from the Marine Corps online. She and I began talking and she was raving about her job and wanted me to come up and visit. She told me I should apply because they had seasonal positions that were coming available just before Christmas. This was shortly before Thanksgiving, and even though I needed a job, my confidence and faith in interviewing had been torn.

A few months prior, I had been interviewed and hired for a position as an accounts payable specialist. The hiring manager hired me and, on the first day, I showed up in a black suit, hair pulled back in a tight bun, nice black pumps, an emerald green shirt to liven up the black, and subtle make-up and jewelry - very professional. The hiring manager greeted me, quickly delivering me to the accounting department manager. The manager began showing me around. Within 20 minutes, I was sitting at what would be my desk and speaking with my supervisor, who would show me my day-to-day tasks. After about 30 minutes, the owner of the company came in and asked to speak with me. Of course, I followed her. Our conversation started out very general and polite, but it was uncomfortable and I felt very uneasy. Well, the owner told me to look around at the people in the company. She then told me that I don't fit in and I'm not what they are looking for in an employee. She had the security guard escort me out of the building. Needless to say, I was crushed and hurt. I sat in the parking lot and cried for an hour.

Now, my friend was asking me to visit 700 miles away from home and apply at a company that I knew very little about. I decided to give it a try. I had nothing to lose, I was already at the bottom. With the little money I had, I flew up and interviewed with Debbie. I was nervous and didn't know how the interview went. I was staying for a couple of days and figured if

I didn't hear anything before I went to Florida, I could at least say that I visited Virginia Beach. On the day that I was preparing to leave, I received a phone call from Debbie. She told me that they really liked me, but couldn't hire me for the position that I applied for. She began to explain to me that it was a seasonal position and since I lived in Florida, it would not be good for me to move so far away from home, having a seasonal position. Once again, I felt defeated, but Debbie wasn't finished. Debbie told me that they had another position that they wanted to offer me. It was full-time, with benefits, and they thought that I would be the perfect fit. I was being hired to manage Online Support. They were giving me a chance. I was ecstatic! Debbie asked if I could move here and start work before Christmas. I didn't know how I could do that, but I agreed.

On December 15, 2008, my life changed as I began to work for Liberty Tax Service. I worked as the Online Support Manager for 2 ½ years, and then another manager recognized my talent and brought me to the Online Products team to work as a business analyst, which I performed for 2 years, until recently being promoted to Project Manager. Liberty gave me an opportunity to grow and find a career that I love. My children live in a home that we are purchasing, and my faith in people and authority has changed. Liberty gave my heart a chance to heal and see that every one of another race, in authority, is not prejudiced or racist. Everyone in this company who has promoted, encouraged, and pushed me to do and be more has been of a different ethnic group other than my own. Everyone is not blessed to find and be given the opportunity to have mentors and a career, but I have been, and for that I am very thankful. Anytime

there is a decision that needs to be made, that I can influence, I remember that Liberty has been loyal to me and I am, therefore, loyal to Liberty.

I am a Liberty Fanatic!

By Joy Pacella/Marketing - Liberty Corporate

When I had my first interview at Liberty Corporate, I thought to myself, going back to corporate America? However, when I walked into the lobby of 1716 Corporate Landing, everyone that walked past was so nice, as they all greeted me. It actually felt like a small company with big ideas and a passion for what was being created inside of the walls of the building.

About six months after I started working here, our CMO, Martha O'Gorman recruited me onto her team in marketing and I haven't looked back. We are very active in community relationships, especially Relay for Life. This is something Martha got me involved in, as these partnerships are important to the success of our company. It's not anything I had ever done before but something I will continue to do forever.

As a 14-year cancer survivor, Relay for Life has a special place in my heart. I had never spoken to anyone about my cancer, for I considered it my burden. Since I have been at Liberty and gotten involved in Relay, I found out that cancer is something to talk about and to be proud that I did survive. I celebrate with others who are fighting and mourn the ones we have lost. I love that Liberty allows us to fundraise, participate, and be active in our community.

Being involved in the community and out in the public is something I never liked to do. At our first event, I put on the costume, handed out crowns and worked in the crowd that I would have otherwise avoided. Liberty changed my life. Because of the community events I can talk to strangers, I can handle working the crowds. I even made a speech at a March of Dimes lunch. It was awesome. Liberty has allowed me to grow as a person and to have more confidence in myself. Liberty allows employees to be themselves and I feel like I am a part of the 2020 vision. My name is Joy. I am a Liberty Fanatic.

It's Our Company

By Jeffrey Brown/Supply, Facilities and
Vendor Relations - Liberty Corporate

At one point, John Hewitt had a mouse problem in his office. It was my job to set the mousetraps and try to catch these little buggers. When I was leaving John's office, I told him, "I love working for your company." John replied, "It's our company." I've never forgotten that.

Now, whenever I talk about Liberty Tax Service, I say, "It's our company." And it really is.

My Dream of Ownership

By Mary Jane DeJaager/Director of Seasonal
Relationships & Company Stores - Liberty Corporate

It was November 1998 and I was working in retail management. I was actually dreading the upcoming "Holiday Season!" Holiday shoppers can often be the "worst" and really don't get the true spirit of Christmas, so I was actually shopping around for a change in career path myself, when I read these words in the Help Wanted section of the newspaper.

Manager wanted, will train, potential ownership call XXX-XXX-XXXX.

I couldn't pick up the phone fast enough; I wanted to be an "OWNER"!!! So began my journey with Liberty Tax Service as an office manager in Leavittsburg, OH. I've been an employee for close to 16 years but, more importantly, I'll be an owner of Liberty Tax Service the rest of my life. There aren't enough words to describe where I've been on this journey, but with a few choice words, you will understand.

I've met business partners from all over the USA/Canada and Puerto Rico. I've had First Class Seating, Five Star restaurants, Multi-Diamond resorts, Eiffel Tower, Caribbean, dozens of Key Note speakers within a hands reach, that I've been privileged to listen to! I've learned how to invest money, save money, and make business decisions that will affect me throughout the rest of my life. They can't teach you these things in even the best MBA programs in the world!!!

I grew up on a farm in a very rural area of Ohio and learned exceptional work ethics from my parents, however, it was always expected that you work harder - not smarter. You didn't need a strong mind as much as you did a strong back to get the job done! My parents believed that hard work would pay off in the long run. They were right in one respect, because the farm was paid off eventually, though they never got to live a good life. They took a 5-day vacation with us once the entire time we grew up. They constantly worried about paying the bills and prayed that the life insurance could take care of us if something happened. I am one of eight siblings so there wasn't much to go around! My parents are the best and I couldn't ask for better parents, but the farm owned them and made them worried about money their entire lives!

I resolved early in life that I didn't want to be worried financially my whole life. I wanted to be a part of something that is much more valuable and wouldn't cost me endless nights of worry, like a farm full of animals! Learning from the elite group of employees and franchisees at Liberty Tax Service has helped me take my dreams of ownership to a new level! I still work very hard as an employee and as an owner of Liberty Tax. I am constantly striving to learn and take each team member and franchisee to a new level financially and professionally! I take my ownership seriously and it is my duty to pay it forward every day! My dream of "Potential Ownership" is a reality! I stand proud and say, I own a piece of Liberty Tax Service, which will be Number 1 in the Universe in 2020!

Our Clients Love Us Back

By Nicole Bellenfant/Zee - Knoxville, TN

My mom is a beautiful person who travels to Knoxville, Tennessee from Chattanooga, every year, and works for me for free. She works from 9am to 9pm EVERY SINGLE day. Last year, however, she was not able to finish.

Today, my mom answered the phone at an office she does not normally work in and answered a question from a client. He then asked, "Is this Judy?" She said, "Yes, it is. Can I help you?" He asked, "How is your mother doing?" She said she is doing much better, thank you, who is this?" He explained who he was and told her he had been praying for my grandmother every single day since last year when she broke her hip and my mom had to return to Chattanooga to care for her. He said, "I promise you not a day has gone past, since I last talked to you, that I haven't asked the

Lord to heal and care for your mother." My mom is the person who usually cares and loves on my clients and so she was so humbled and overwhelmed by our customer's actions, she was moved to tears.

We have the best clients on the planet who are not only loyal, but have taken us into their hearts as much as we have taken them into ours! What a wonderful business we are blessed to be in!

My American Dream

By Craig Comer/Zee - Detroit, MI

When I went into business for myself in the fall of 2002, I held a firm belief in investing in my employees, which included mentoring them and enriching their lives as best as I could. "The more you give, the more you get," is a saying that was passed on to me by one of my life mentors. To this day, I believe even more in that philosophy. I have truly experienced the American Dream of owning a successful business. As a result, I feel it is important to give back and help those that have allowed me to experience that dream. The following stories are some examples.

A few years ago, I helped advise a key manager on how to improve her credit from a score that was so low she could not even open a bank account. After a year of planning and executing some ideas that I had learned from a banker friend, she was able to purchase the first home of her life at age 29. That was something that no one in her family had been able to do before her.

Each year, I have taken key employees to the Liberty convention for fun, celebration, and learning. This is an investment of time and money that has paid off in ways I could not predict. The employees have made friends and key contacts in the Liberty family that will last a lifetime and help them grow professionally within their Liberty career. In 2013, we made a 13-hour road trip from Detroit to Virginia Beach. We stopped in Washington D.C. to see the White House and other sites on a beautiful spring day and had lunch in front of the Lincoln Memorial. We also went to a Detroit Tigers road baseball game in Baltimore, and witnessed history as they hit three home runs in a row. None of the key employees along on the trip had ever been to a major league baseball game or to our nation's

Capitol. One employee had never been out of the Detroit area in her life. It was a memorable trip to say the least.

I have been there for employees in a time of need, such as when a manager did not have heat because her furnace broke before tax season. She had purchased the house earlier in the year to live close to the store she managed, and had spent countless hours rehabbing and fixing the property through the summer and fall. However, she did not have the money to pay for the large repair just before tax season began. I provided a furnace contractor and negotiated to pay him in advance for the work to be completed. I had also donated several household items to assist her in rehabbing her home. The same manager's car was severely damaged in our parking lot during tax season and was not drivable. Naturally, this happened during peak week, but I was able to loan her my car so that she could get to work and supervise her three stores. She was very grateful for all of this help. I am very grateful for her hard work and passion at Liberty.

Three years ago, I started a 401(k) plan with company matching for key employees. My dad was a financial planner for educators. From an early age, he taught me the importance of saving money for the future. Not only will I pass this lesson on to my children, but feel it is important to educate key employees and give them the necessary tools to do this for themselves and their families.

These are examples of many stories of how I give back to the people who take pride in what they do personally and at Liberty. With all of the negativities in life and our society, it feels rewarding to have good people in my life, and to be able to help and take care of them as best I can. It is a part of my American Dream.

The Greatest Place to Work

By Amanda N. Johnson/Office Manager - Kinston, NC

I had recently moved from Illinois to North Carolina during the winter of 2011. Jobs were scarce, and it was unexpectedly difficult to adjust and become familiar with the culture of the South. I felt very far away from home, very discouraged, and very out of place. One day, I was out job searching, and I passed the Liberty Tax office in Kinston, NC. I saw a sign that read, "Get Paid To Wave." I called the office and was invited to come in and fill out an application, and "try out" for the job. I came to the try-outs and, though it was fun, I wasn't picked to be a waver. I had never seen a tax office like Liberty before. There were applicants present who possessed (what young people call) "mad" dance skills; needless to say, they outshined me (I'm barely capable of pulling off the mashed potato).

I enrolled in an associate degree program later that year, and began my studies in accounting. The following fall, I saw an ad in the newspaper for Tax School. I called the number listed and signed up to attend an 8-week tax course. I was hired to be a tax preparer for the 2013 tax season. I really enjoyed preparing taxes, but once the tax season had ended, I continued with my studies and went to work in a factory. I had every intention of returning next year to prepare taxes with Liberty again. It was a great experience.

When the tax season had ended for 2013, the owner, Wendy Rhodes, had us fill out a survey. We were encouraged to write suggestions or ideas for the office/business. I wrote down everything I could think of. Though I worried I would be perceived as annoying, I took the chance anyway. A few months later, Wendy called me and asked if I planned to come back for the tax season. She asked me if I would be willing to help get things shaken up (so to speak) for the next tax year, as well as be willing to teach the fall tax classes. I agreed, and enjoyed every single moment of the fall tax season. We kicked off the year with a great start, and ended up being #1 in our district after the first peak. We worked really hard pre-season to build a great team, as well as implement changes that would assist all of us in providing great customer service to Liberty clients.

After my marriage ended, I struggled many years to provide for my three children and myself. I've worked as many as three jobs at one time. I've lost my hair, my home, and my hope that I would ever again find happiness in the everyday tasks and obligations of life. Liberty has created an avenue of expression for me in that I have been able to affect change and prosperity by sharing from my own life experiences. It is a sincere pleasure to give back to my fellow employees and the company owner, as well as the Kinston community. This is the greatest place to work in the country (and I suppose Canada, too). We are real people, affecting real lives, and our success is already built on the firm foundation of the Liberty Corporate values. I have the sincerest gratitude, appreciation, and respect for this company, my boss, and my fellow co-workers. I expect nothing but good things for our future!

The Culture of Winning

By Chris Bushey/Assistant VP of
Franchise Operations - Liberty Corporate

Immediately after graduating from college, I started working at Liberty Tax at the age of 23. During my 14 years at Liberty, I have often thought about what brought me here, what has kept me here, and what keeps me consistently motivated to drive myself and the company toward success. The answer that is most compelling is the culture that the company has created around being a winner. It is the classic David and Goliath story. The odds can be against you, the competition can be formidable, and the detractors can be many, but none of that matters if you are focused on the steps required to tackle that challenge and come out on the other side as a winner.

I started with Liberty in our Mapping Department, worked in Technical Support, and then transitioned to the Director of Supply where I also was the Chairman for our National Convention. I was then given the opportunity to move into the Operations Department where I progressed to the Director of Canadian Franchise Operations and now to the Assistant VP of Operations. I was one of the inaugural members of our Culture Committee, and I continue to strive to keep our culture at the forefront of our company.

A company's culture is the glue that binds things together, and it's the hardest thing for a competitor to copy. This has been an amazing journey, and while many things have changed during my time with the company, the one thing that has remained consistent has been the idea that success is the direct result of taking the right actions, doing things the right way at the right time, and for the right reasons. This is what has catapulted us to where we are today and is what will push us to our goals in the future. Everyone wants to be a part of a winning team, and I've been blessed with that opportunity my entire professional career.

Liberty Has Taken Me from Employee to Employer!

By Tami Karnes/Zee - Bourne, TX

My journey with Liberty Tax began back in 2005, when I found myself relocated to a new state and a new town where I only knew one family. I had made the move under the impression that there was going to be a job for me in the Property Management Software industry that I had been working in for the past several years. To say that the job fell through after I made the move would be an understatement! Scared and unemployed, I saw a Liberty Tax Service office getting ready to open down the street from my house. I had taken a tax preparation class and had been self-employed as a tax preparer for over 10 years at that time, so I decided to give it a shot.

Stopping by the office resulted in my being offered the Office Supervisor/Tax School Instructor position with this brand new Liberty Tax Franchisee, starting immediately - I was thrilled! Thus the journey began. I immediately fell in love with the Liberty Culture, the Mission Statement, and the vision of Liberty Tax!

I remained with this franchise for the next 3 years and just loved it. Subsequently, I was offered other job in another city and moved away to take that position, which I worked at for the next 2+ years. The economy took a real hit on non-profits and I was downsized in 2011. Two days after losing that job, I was scouring Craigslist looking for the next opportunity and saw that the local Liberty Tax office was seeking an Office Supervisor - what an amazing blessing! The post had only been up for a couple of hours, so I called and was hired immediately due to my previous Liberty Tax experience. The next 2 1/2 years had me right back on the Liberty Tax bandwagon and I helped to breathe life back into a failing location - it was exhilarating!

My small town community really rallied behind our efforts to reestablish this location that had been poorly run and managed the previous year. In those short 2 1/2 years, I went through 3 different franchise owners and struggled with a poor location. Then came the news in April of 2013 - the franchise was being sold back to corporate! Thankfully, corporate retained me as the Office Supervisor, but now the franchise was up for sale.

Every effort that I made to try to purchase the franchise myself fell flat - I didn't have any money and previous issues with shaky credit made it a tough road. I prayed, I pleaded, I cried, I felt completely desperate to make this franchise my own and move from being an employee to being an employer! Thank God for answered prayers! A small group of friends and family joined together and contributed the operating capital that would be needed to get us into tax season and corporate agreed to finance the franchise fees and we closed on November 18, 2013! Priority 1 became to move the location from the failing spot at the north end of town and get back to the South side in time for tax season. We took possession of the new location on December 18 and hit the ground running; calling every customer from the past year to make sure they knew that we had moved. The community support of the new location and the wonderful opportunity given to me to move from being an employee to an employer has been phenomenal!!

Our new location is beautiful and our numbers are up a solid 40% from this time last tax season! I can't thank Liberty Tax enough for having faith in me and being willing to help me make this franchise my own and bring it back to its former glory - my life is forever changed thanks to Liberty Tax Service!!

I Love My New Life

Lashundra Ard/Tax Preparer - Columbia, MS

Fanatic! Liberty called me in September 2013 & asked was I interested in Tax School. Dreams do come true! I have always wanted to become a tax preparer. They trained me professionally & hired me. I must say that being able to experience what you hoped for is life changing. I love my new life. Thank you, Liberty!

Liberty Will Always Be a Part of My Family

Linda Lizotte/Senior Tax Preparer - Charlotte, NC

I have worked for Liberty Tax Service for seven years as a Senior Tax Preparer. I have enjoyed working for Kay Weldon in North Carolina. I look forward to work each and every day. As a Senior Tax Preparer, I have worked long hours and work every day, while attending college full time.

I am currently working toward my MBA in accounting, with a specialty in taxation. This will help Liberty Tax with more complex taxes, especially corporations and estate taxes. Liberty Tax will always be part of my family.

Surrounded by Passionate People

By Malissa Greenwood/Marketing/PR Manager - Casper, WY

I worked for Liberty Tax Casper, WY several years ago as a Tax Preparer. I remember seeing how hard working and passionate the owner, Sandy S., was. She was constantly making herself available to customers, answering questions, contacting the IRS for clients and regularly putting in 12+ hour days to ensure that every need was met. It blew me away that she was always ready and willing to help people even if they had gotten their taxes done somewhere else!

It was because of this example of work ethic that I came back this year, but this time as the local Marketing/PR Manager. Today, Sandy is still the same! But she's also built an amazing team full of Tax Preparers who share her passion, attention to detail, and motivation to create raving fans!

For just one example, Tax Preparer and Manager, Carmen M., has spent countless hours reaching out to the Hispanic community – leading seminars, helping them understand the ITIN process, why they need to get one, and then helping them with both current and previous year's taxes. She is one of the only people in the entire community to do this! Now, while I don't speak Spanish, I can understand a smile and a happy customer in any language!

The entire staff has been onboard and helpful with promoting all the fundraisers we've done too, knowing that the most important part of those days is giving back to the community we live in. Working in this kind of helpful, educational, and fanatical environment makes my job very easy. It's definitely not hard to advertise and reach out to the community when you are surrounded by passionate people, ready go above and beyond for literally anyone that walks through the door!

I Never Looked Back

Mary Jo Armstrong/Zee - Natrona Heights & Kittanning, PA

I was a stay-at-home mom for nine years. I loved being one, but my husband was very abusive. He had rages daily. I just loved the time with my children and if I left, I would lose that time being there when they grew up. I have a Master's degree in Mechanical Engineering, but with that job I would be away from my kids a lot because it was very demanding and a lot of traveling.

I stayed also because I was afraid of him getting any kind of custody. I needed to be certain that they would never have to be alone with him.

The year before I left, I cared for my mom who was dying of cancer. She was such a strong and amazing women. I would do anything for her, as she would me. She was the love of my dad's life and his anchor. Dad completely lost his mind to Alzheimer's disease when she was dying. He could not handle the stress of it. He leaned on my mom even more after my only other sibling, my sister, died of cancer nine years earlier. During this time, I was very preoccupied with my parents. This allowed my husband to be abusive to my children. My girls normally would tell me that he was being mean, but they were so worried about me and the stress I had over my parents, that they lied to me and said he was being nice. I thought maybe since I wasn't around, he was being nice.

I started noticing my 8-year-old daughter's face getting a pale, grayish look. I kept thinking she was sick, later I found out that she has severe Post Traumatic Stress Disorder from her dad's yelling. On Dec. 22, that same daughter got a severe head injury at school. She had debilitating headaches and would pass out daily.

Hours later, my mom died.

My dad would just drive around in circles. Going to his favorite restaurant, ordering the same thing up to five times a day now. His mind was completely gone. January 9th, just weeks after my Mom died, my husband threatened my life and grabbed my sick daughter and said some horrible things to her. I called the police and got the needed protection from abuse. I never looked back.

Now I had to get a job... Wow. My Mom just died. My Dad is completely uncontrollable at this time and needs some immediate attention from me. My daughters and I all had severe PTSD from the abuse. My one daughter, at times, is actually paralyzed from the combination of the head injury and the PTSD. When she would think of her Dad, she literally could not walk. She was extremely sick and needed daily therapy. How the heck am I going to support myself, I wondered?

My mom left me some money. I used that to start my Liberty Tax business. For me, there was nothing else I would want to do. My dad was an accountant and I remember being able to go to his office and go to work with him because he owned the business. I also remember many family vacations because tax season was short and he had the summer basically free for us. Liberty allowed me to be able to schedule my own work time. I was able to take care of my dad when I needed to, and I was able to take my daughter to therapy. I eventually took my children out of school because of the concussion. Wow, my girls saw me stand up after years of abuse and start my own business! What a great gift to give them!

Also, going back to work, I wanted to do something that I felt good about at the end of the day and that was Fun, like when I was a stay-at-home mom. Liberty gave me that! I am so appreciative! My children and I collected food for food drives, gave free returns to people in need, did blood drives and did a fundraiser for our local abuse center. Thanks to Liberty, I joined the Chamber of Commerce. The president of the Chamber recommended me to be on the board of the HOPE Center (which is our abuse center). I now can help other people who were in my situation and show them that through Liberty I survived and so can they! I also give free returns to the residents at the center every year. Also, giving the refund checks to people brings me so much joy. They are so excited! So many of our clients don't have cars. They go and buy them with their refund checks and are so excited! I just love being part of that!

Liberty gave me a job in which I could be associated with people of very high morals and one I am proud of. I know I am making my community a better place because of Liberty. I am teaching my girls lessons. It also gave me time for my family. Plus, we have the best CEO - John! I am very proud to be part of his organization!! :)

God Answers Prayers, and Liberty was Part of Our Answer!

Todd & Karen Swicegood/Multi-Unit Zees - NC

June 28th, 2012... our fourth year of marriage, both from very expensive divorces. I had been a very successful financial advisor my entire career. My wife had been a mother, and realtor. We both were living under tremendous strains from divorce costs, integrating families and were still feeling the affects of 2008's financial crisis.

I was in the office alone one morning, it was quiet and I was praying for guidance, direction and a new path for my wife and me. While I was praying, my computer email indicator pinged. I finished my prayer, and began my workday. I opened my email, and the email that was sitting there was a marketing email from Liberty about tax franchises.

Purely happenstance? Maybe. If you are a believer, and my wife and I both are, you have to believe it was more than coincidence. But I didn't listen. I went right on pursuing my day. Over the weekend, I did some more research. I discussed it with my wife, and she was adamantly against it. As many great relationships are, she and I are different on the risk-taking front. Ultimately, we pursued via the email.

We met Kendra Williams. She set us up for a visit at Liberty Tax in Virginia Beach. There we went through the introduction and first met John Hewitt. At that time, we found out that the two towns I operated in both had offices that were for sale and had a fairly significant stream of income already… another answer to prayers.

We were working to take on a partner, but he backed away. We felt we had already agreed on price and were committed to becoming Liberty Franchisees. We finished our first year with our offices up over 25% and made Top Gun. We knew we were in the right place.

What a new life that opened up for us. We have met some wonderful people. Scott & Christy Curtis, the AD in our southern region, Ryan & Tiffany Dodson in our northern region, have become great friends, partners and helpful Area Developers. David & Jamie Schuck, Elite 18 members have become friends and mentors. Our world has opened up.

The great thing about Liberty Tax is that you can come with financial stresses and find financing which can allow you to begin rebuilding your financial life, where otherwise you could not have. Again we were out of divorces, very expensive divorces. Credit was tight; capital was not available. John Hewitt looks out and sees people willing to work hard and follow the Liberty motto of: Set the Standard, Improve Each Day and Have Some Fun.

Today we have 7 offices, should do close to 4,000 tax returns in year 2015, and see a bright and shining retirement business that we are building fast! We intend to focus on the 2020 vision and have 15 offices by 2020 with 15,000 tax returns. Our prayer for direction was answered!

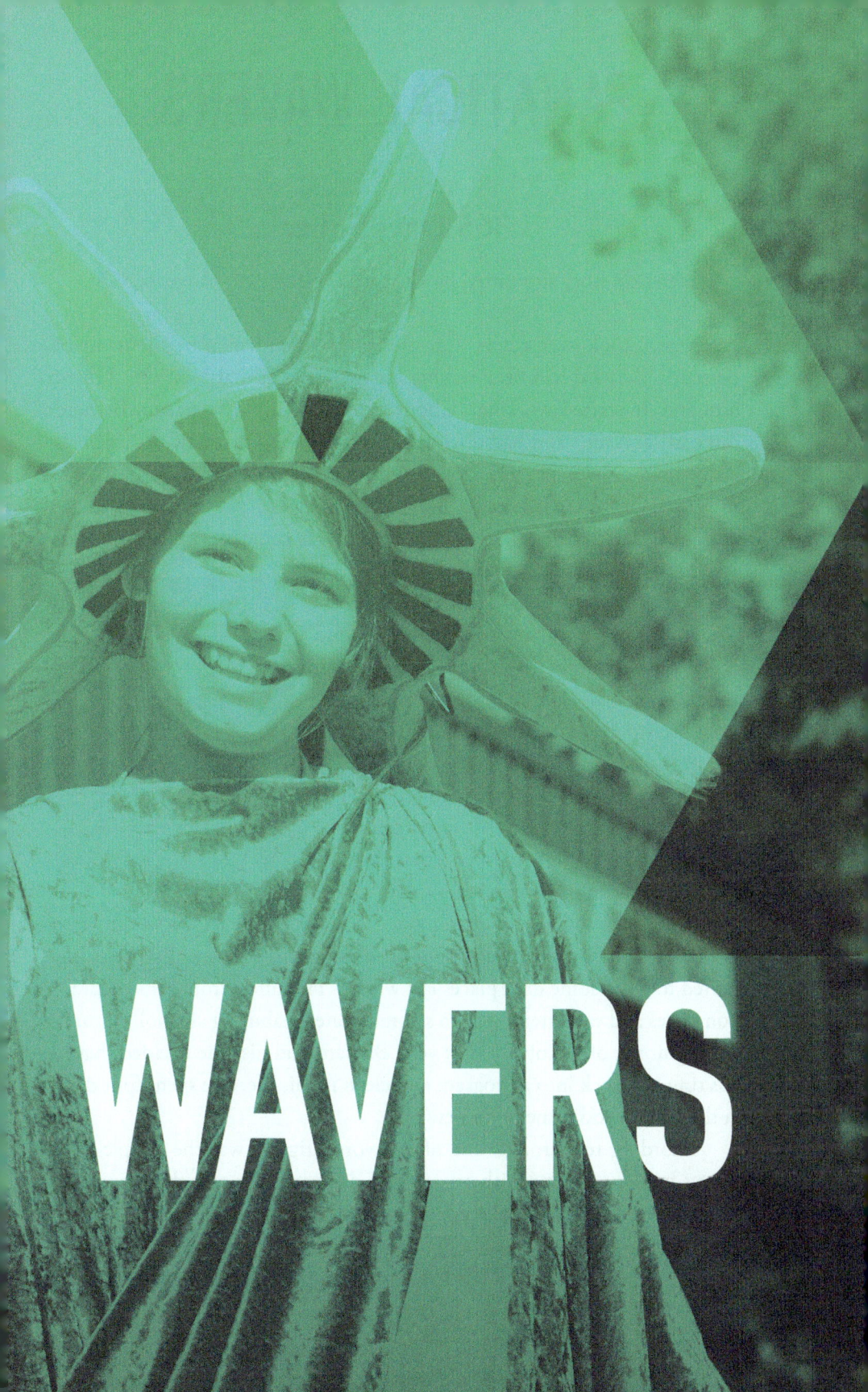

FANATICAL WAVERS

365 Days Sober

Bernard's story submitted by Cuylor Leverett/ Zee - Augusta, GA

Last year, I took over a new store and hired a gentleman by the name of Bernard. Bernard had been waving for two years at that location. I hired him and he started working. About two weeks into the season, Bernard came in for a shift and had obviously been drinking that day. As much as it hurt to do, we let Bernard go.

Last fall, we started seeing Bernard hanging around the area as usual, but he seemed a little different than before. He came in several times and asked for his job back. Initially, I told him no, but Bernard is a go-getter. He is relentless. He finally came to my manager, Bill Kemp, and explained to Bill that he was sober, cleaned up, and ready to work. Bill told him that we would try to give him another chance.

In the coming weeks, every time Bernard came by he had a new number to tell us. His number went from 30 to 40 to 50 and continued to climb. This number - that Bernard wears as a badge of courage every day - is his number of days sober. I decided to talk to Bernard and get the whole story so that we could help him and support him on this journey. Bernard's life started to go to some dark places last winter. He suffers from some depression issues and was attempting to self medicate by abusing alcohol. Around the beginning of October of last year, Bernard and his wife decided that it was time to check into a program and clean up his life. He spent four days in the facility and came out a new man.

According to Bernard, one of his worst triggers was the people that he was hanging around with on a day-to-day basis. He says that now Liberty has given him somewhere to be around positive people who support him instead of bringing him down. In his words "Liberty is a blessing. I get to see smiling faces and how people light up to see me waving."

Bernard's initial goal is to make it to 365 days sober. Every day, his family asks him what is his number? Every day, his Liberty family also asks him what is his number? Bernard is a new man. This morning, Bill asked, "Bernard what's your number?" Today, Bernard's number is 110.

High School Senior Loves Liberty!

By Juliette Sykes/Zee - Midlothian, VA

These days, we hear so much bad news about kids. Well, Tara Custalow and our team of fanatical wavers are the exception. Tara is a senior in high school, who works non-stop because she loves Liberty Tax.

As a waver, she dances her heart out; she inspires people! Some folks stop just to watch her dance or give her hot chocolate. On her break, she still doesn't stop – she finds things to do, like helping to clean the office. Tara will use her 10-minute break to label envelopes or anything else that needs to be done. We have six seniors on our waver team and they also coordinate with each other to make sure the shifts are covered. Can you believe that? On Martin Luther King Day, when many kids enjoyed the day off, Tara helped me on business-to-business marketing. She loves it! She tells business owners, "this is reverse Halloween – I wear the costume and you get the candy."

In the off-season, Tara calls me or emails to see if I need anything. Last November, she put together all of my goodie bags and helped me make calls for tax school. Tara's mom works as our receptionist, and Tara is hoping to get her 16-year-old sister involved with Liberty.

The confidence she's gained at Liberty has also helped her tackle challenges in her own life. Tara found the motivation to get her learner's permit to start driving, and I can't wait to see how she continues to grow and succeed. Tara is truly fanatical about Liberty!

$1000 in Cash!

By Deb Prior/Zee - Manchester, CT

My waver, Brenda, who is in wheelchair, has been working for me for the past three tax seasons. Each year she gets better and better. When she saw me come into the office today, she motorized her scooter/chair into the office, all excited. With tears in her eyes, she handed me a card and said, "Look what a lady stopped and gave me today!" I can't remember the exact words in the card, but it was something like, "You smile at people every day and bless their day. You are truly blessed, too."

Inside the card was an envelope with $1,000 in cash!

Wow, huh?

Liberty is Everywhere!

By Fred Bach/District Manager - Sacramento, CA

In Lodi, California, we have a waver who has his own motto: "Liberty is Everywhere!" His name is Phil Maynard and he's brand new to us. Phil borrowed a costume and danced at different monuments in the area, promoting Liberty on his own time.

People come into the store just because of him, and Phil says Liberty also changed his life. His application for the job was to show us a video of himself dancing in another costume he borrowed. When Phil's on the job, you can see people smiling, waving, and hear horns honking as he spins the sign.

Phil is not only fanatical, he's everywhere!

Willis the Waver Makes Us #1

By Andrew Banker/Zee-Area Developer, Kansas City

Willis Tyrus started with me 10 years ago, and he's the reason we're the number one office in Kansas City. The *Wall Street Journal* first profiled

Willis, getting us national press, and local news loves him too! He's been featured on many "pay it forward," segments.

Willis is the best waver I've ever had; the most energy and enthusiasm I've ever seen! Here's what's so special – Willis is a senior citizen in his late 60's, who walks with a cane. He only missed one year with me because he had a stroke. Willis consistently gets more tips and compliments than any waver I've ever known.

There is only one word for Willis: phenomenal!

A Big Man with a Heart of Gold

By Nancy S Hall/Zee & Area Developer, CPA - Southern Arizona

Carroll works for a carnival and has been a waver for a couple of years. He called me for his old job back. However, he was in Benson, AZ and needed to get gas money and drive 60 miles to move his travel trailer to Tucson. I told him as soon as he arrived in Tucson, come to work.

He is a very big man with a heart of gold. He will help us in any way; a truly nice person.

The other day he went back out to wave after taking a break. A woman came up to him and asked if she could take his picture. He said that was fine. He likes to get us publicity. The woman then gave him a wad of money and a note saying her father had died, and wanted his money given out. $100!

So guess what Carroll did? He put it in the bank (right in our shopping center) and the next day came to work with donuts for everyone.

It was nice to see affirmation of what comes around, goes around. Even though Carroll doesn't have much for himself, he's always thinking of how he can give back to others.

We're a Family!

By Tina Litkenhus/Marketing Manager - Lawrenceburg, KY

Hands down, we have the greatest group of wavers in Lawrenceburg, Kentucky. Why? Because just like a family, they take care of each other. Some of our wavers don't have vehicles and need to walk one or two miles to the job. As much as possible, wavers try to coordinate rides to help each other get to work. Our wavers return year after year. Most have been with us for the last couple of years.

We have a spirit of camaraderie and a family atmosphere here. We are a team and we teach policies and procedures to every employee. Everything Liberty corporate sends to help us run our business works, and we share it with the entire team. We tell our wavers that they are just as important as our tax preparers. There is no separation here – we are in this together.

We call Diane our hula-hoop girl. She works at a horse farm and is used to being outside. She has quite a following in our community! She keeps a supply of hula-hoops on hand because clients are always asking to buy them from her and for lessons. She bought a glowing hula-hoop for night waving, and sometimes performs with two at a time.

We also have a husband and wife team (Ryan and Christa) who really add to our family atmosphere. Then there's David. On his own time, he pitches in to shovel out front, unload soda and water, or clean our wagon. He does this without being asked.

Jessica is new to our team and walks to work, unless another waver can drive her. She also loves this position and our family. The caring and compassion shown among this group of wavers is truly FANATICAL.

Fanatical Energy!

By Emmanuel Teferi/Zee - Granite City, IL

My name is Emmanuel Teferi, franchise owner from the Granite City location in Illinois. My father and I are in our first year together in the tax business and we purchased a corporate-owned store. Being a turnkey operation, we were fortunate to inherit a great group of people, including some excellent three-year wavers.

But one waver in particular is above and beyond!!! His name is William Carruba. He actually came in last year to do his taxes for the first time. The lead preparer worked with him and said that William was a hoot!!! He has an infectious personality that is truly genuine, despite many obstacles. He is outgoing and truly wants to grow with our new team. As a customer last year, he was making everyone in the office laugh. He even wanted to put on the store's big "Liberty head," and dance around, so they let him!! Our lead preparer couldn't stop laughing, and put some pictures on the Liberty Facebook page last year.

With that being said, he came in this year and wanted a job as a waver. Everyone in our turnkey operation remembered him, so without hesitation, we hired him on the spot. He is more than a waver; his positive energy has even carried on to my marketing efforts. He has done some business-to-business marketing with me and did a great job for a beginner. He also set up an appointment for me with the Ford dealership to possibly have a waver in the background of their commercial. Stay tuned!

William just celebrated his 21st birthday and his fanatical energy is non-stop!

Waving at People, Not Cars

By Doug Hicks/Zee - Wichita, KS

Here in Wichita, Kansas at our South Broadway location, we are very interested in helping those that life has dealt a rough hand and giving back whenever possible. We have a relationship with placement specialists at COMCARE, a state run organization that assists the mentally challenged in finding housing and employment. We have hired four of their clients as wavers. Most of these people worked over the Christmas season as Salvation Army bell ringers! They are not afraid of the rough Kansas winters and they are excited to have jobs!

A good example is Shawn; he works our early shift. He catches his bus at 5:30 in the morning and arrives ready for work about ten minutes before 7:00. He is very proud that he puts out all of our American flags and wind feathers in the morning. He walks in for his break and boasts, "I wave at the people, not at the cars. Cars don't file tax returns!" He is back on station after 10 minutes, dancing and waving and he keeps his energy up and smiles for his entire shift.

We feel good that we have the opportunity to know great people like Shawn, who are working to become productive members of our community.

Kevin Gets His Groove On

By Bob Shin/Zee - Colorado Springs, CO

Kevin Wright loves to get his groove on the minute he puts on his Lady Liberty costume! He is from the great state of Hawaii, and he was raised mostly in Los Angeles, California. Apart from waving for Liberty Tax in Colorado Springs – Austin Bluffs, he works as a conductor on the Cog Rail train that travels up to the summit of Pikes Peak, more than 14,000 feet high.

Kevin has training in ballroom and salsa dancing and he loves to play midnight (indoor) soccer after working his five hour shifts with Liberty. Kevin is extremely physically fit, a constant ball of energy, and he attracts great attention for the store. On one occasion, one of our preparers witnessed a fire truck going to an emergency call with its lights & sirens and one of the firemen noticed Kevin dancing on the corner of Austin Bluffs and Academy Blvd, one of the busiest intersections in Colorado Springs. Even though they were in route to an emergency call, this fireman took the time to extend his body outside the window of the fire truck and wave back at Kevin.

On another occasion, two females approached Kevin after witnessing his fabulous dance moves and asked if he needed a dance partner. As professional as Kevin is, he stated, "Sure as long as you don't do anything crazy, I'm working right now." Last week, another female called the office and asked one of the tax preparers if Kevin was single! Not only is Kevin a chick magnet, he has been a great employee for Liberty. He always shows up for his shift and has been very punctual. Kevin embraces the Liberty vision and understands that he and our other wavers are the front line for our store, especially during first peak.

We are proud and honored to have him as an employee!

Greg Epitomizes What a Waver Should Be

By Nicole Morgan/Office Supervisor - Williamsburg, Virginia

Greg Galland heard about Liberty Tax from a friend of his. He had seen people do the "waver thing," and he thought it would be a really fun job. His friend mentioned that Liberty needed wavers, and I can tell you that he blew away the audition, even volunteering to dance in the snow!

Greg's background in theater makes him perfect for the job. Not long after he started, he made headlines in the local paper because of his enthusiasm. He was making drivers laugh, and bringing the customers in one-by-one. They couldn't stop talking about what a great job he was doing.

After his first year, Greg decided that this was the best job because he got to be himself. He got to show his energy, and being a waver allowed him to be excited and have tons a fun (which he says most people do not get to do!). He decided to come back the second year and prove, yet again, to be the perfect waver.

Now, this is his third year as a waver. He's hoping that he will be able to bring in a lot more customers and dance his heart out, so that we can do their taxes. I really think that Greg epitomizes what every waver should set out to be. He is energetic, enthusiastic and, most importantly, passionate about his job. This isn't just another job for him to bring in a little extra cash; it's a reflection of Liberty Tax.

He is by far, the best waver that I have ever seen in the 11 years that I have worked for Liberty Tax. I'm so proud to have Greg as a part of our team here, and his dedication to Liberty Tax is why this company is what it is.

Party on Garden Grove Street!

By Candace Vallarta/Marketing Manager - Garden Grove, CA

The most fanatical waver (that I KNOW is a fanatic) is Louis Herrera from the Garden Grove, California office.

Louis is the best because he's not just fanatical on the job; he's also a fanatic off of work! He attracts tons of attention on the streets. I have seen people come out of their cars, walk up to Louis, and shake his hand for doing such an amazing job! He dances, turns, flips, and throws the sign up in the air. He also plays the harmonica! He sings and always comes to work on time. He even stays after work to help clean and organize the office.

What makes him especially fanatical is his energy, joy, and leadership skills. He takes initiative and is responsible. He's a go-getter, funny, and he's a people magnet! What makes him MOST fanatical of all is his character.

The Most Valuable Wavers

By Kay Cobbs/Zee -Tulsa and Broken Arrow, OK

We have the most valuable wavers! They are two brothers, John & Randy, that started with the company around 2009. They have been back every year since. Randy got his job back with Walmart, and uses his free time to continue waving for us.

John absolutely spoils us! He will make the coffee, if we are too busy; he vacuums without us asking, and takes out the trash. He even asks the customers if they need drinks. About two weeks ago, on a Sunday, he started having blurred vision and was falling down. His brother got him to the emergency room and found out that he had had a minor stroke. His blood pressure was through the roof at 230! He was in the hospital for a week, because it took them that long to get him stabilized and all he wanted to know is if he still had a job! Of course he did!! He received his medical release to go back to work that next Monday after getting out of the hospital on Friday!

He has blurred vision still from the clot in the back of his head, and the doctors are saying his vision should come back in time, but he is still holding that sign for us and still takes care of us!! God Bless our Wavers!!

A Gleaming Personality

By William Daniels/Zee - Houston, TX

I hired a young man named Julio. This year he came in with his parents to get their taxes done. He had a gleaming personality, so I decided to offer him a job on the spot. He watched the waver videos online and instantly said "Yes, I can do that." He was fascinated with sign spinning, as he had never seen anything like that before. He taught himself to be a sign spinner.

Three days later, the phone calls started pouring in from clients saying how awesome he is and from others who wanted to be wavers. Julio has become so awesome at his job. Approximately two weeks after hiring Julio, I had a grand opening and roadside party at one of my new locations. I knew we had to have him there. He was the life of the party and as result of his street performance, he was offered three different job opportunities that day. He turned them all down and is still my waver today.

He is always on time and is so proud of the job. It wasn't until half way into the tax season, that I learned that Julio has a pacemaker. He is so active I became a little nervous having him doing that job. As I talked to him, he told me that he had cleared everything through his doctor and there was nothing else he would rather be doing.

Helping Amy

Mark Meyers/Zee - Schertz, TX

As a new "Zee", I've run into the typical situation of needing to have more wavers than you think you need. Then there is Amy Neubauer. Amy came to my office just as tax season was opening looking for a waver position; she mentioned she had once been a waver in Georgia and was very familiar with responsibilities of the position.

Amy wasn't the most energetic waver I've seen or hired, and certainly wasn't the most acrobatic waver either. In fact, Amy probably wouldn't pass 99.9% of anyone's auditions or tryouts. I still hired Amy because she knew what the Lady Liberty symbol meant, and was committed and dedicated to do as much as she could do when I needed her. Amy has some health issues and she needed a job; she also turned out to be my most dependable, reliable, and professional waver. If my clients say they saw Miss Liberty, it's because they saw Amy.

Helping Amy is just another example of Liberty Tax Service giving something back to the community. My office gets to touch the lives of many people in the communities where I live and serve. Amy's sense of purpose has touched the lives in my office and we're all the better for it.

A Reason to Get Out of Bed in the Mornings

By Patricia Cutrell/Waver - Valdosta, GA

It was two years ago and I was out of a job. I looked each day. I was getting tired, and I cried each day. I asked God to direct me to a job. I saw someone waving and I thought to myself, why not? So I went and applied.

Evonnie and Doug hired me. I didn't work last year, but did this year and I love it. I love people and I love to smile and try to make someone's day. I have been able to put food on the table for my family because of Liberty Tax. They gave me a reason to get out of bed in the mornings.

True Pride and Accomplishment

Michael Chenoweth/Waver - Everett, WA

So I don't really know how to start this, but I guess you could say I was never really a star student. My success didn't really start until later on in life. My family always did the best they could for me. My mother did have some mental & physical handicaps that made it difficult to grasp a normal routine of learning by example, but she loved me and always fought to give it her all before her problems became too severe.

When they did, I went 30 miles east to the Cascade Foot Hills along the beautiful Skykomish River, off of Highway 2 in Gold Bar, Washington. Not many people have heard of it, because it's one of those towns you blink on a road trip and you've missed it. This is where the main pinnacles of life came to fruition for me as a child and partly as an adult.

My grandpa was the greatest thing to a father figure. He taught me most of what I know today and am grateful for every bit of it. When no one else could, he was there to show me how to tie the laces on shoes, ride a bike, and throw a baseball. One of my favorites was fishing. Most importantly, my grandpa was a great example of someone who could work. Now when I say work, he wasn't a paperwork all-nighter guy, or a tool set and car guy, he was kind of something different. For years, I looked up in the sky to see a man who was never afraid of anything.

This man was a logger by trade, excavator on the side, and fisherman all at the same time (literally). I've seen him stop a back hoe, put his climbing gear on to clear a wind fall 60 feet up, and stop for a smoke break to yell down how to reel in a fish, while I was standing on the back deck of a cabin, sitting river front. I could write a book about all that. Later on in life, I'd remember this in pursuing my career.

As a teenager, I fell into a drug addiction to try to escape memories of a not so pleasant city life. By age 16, I'd seen more trauma than most adults would be able to cope with normally. By the time I was 19, I'd combined a drug habit with an equally deadly alcohol recipe. When I was 20, I'd overdosed twice, been to jail three times due to my self affliction and I had no idea how this would impact me in the future, because I didn't really care.

It took me a full year to recover from almost a 10-year addiction. It was a full year and more after my mother died in a horrific accident that I was fully done. I had to start over. The only family still willing to help were my grandparents. They played a big part in my recovery and still do. My grandpa put me to work helping the community with extensive yard work and landscaping. My grandma talked with me and made sure I wasn't going to relapse. I did a couple times when I came back to the city, that's not her fault though.

After awhile, I left to branch out on my own and gained my first job with a company there. I worked a full time summer job as a janitor and ran a machine that cleaned the floors. When that was over, it was time to come back home. A short while afterwards I ran into a man called John Williams in Snohomish, WA. His recruiter for sign wavers showed me one of the training videos and I saw a guy flipping the sign around and doing all this amazing stuff. That's when I looked at her and said, "I can do that." She replied, "Sure you can!" enthusiastically, but I could sense the doubt. After a near broken sign and a lot of embarrassment I was doing that! I'd become a pro.

For the first time, I'd felt true pride and accomplishment, in myself. I took this confidence on to other jobs, back around to Liberty Tax office in Everett. I'm writing all this before I start my shift at 1pm, and I've gained even more skills from working here, as well. I feel it when people honk at me, or give me a thumbs up that - for once - I'm actually good at something. Even though it's temporary, this job is the highlight of my year, and is a strong contribution on having almost four years clean from drugs.

Now, I have a child on the way that I'm super excited about, but scared for at the same time. I don't feel entirely secure with our situation right now, but feel that somehow everything will fall into place.

A Brand New Person

Eric Wynder/Waver - Hampton, VA

One day, I was searching the Craigslist employment website and saw that Liberty Tax Service was hiring for wavers. So I went in and was asked to dance. So I danced, and she said I hoped you could dance and do a little more. I said yes. So I started the next day and started to dance and got a lot of comments saying he does very well and he's different, and does more than just wave. He engages and if they ask him to dance, he dances all over Hampton, Virginia.

My life has changed a lot because of the lady that took me under her wing (her name is Giselle Robinson). So she noticed, and Ms. Vanetta asked if I needed something to eat. They fed me and they never took it out of my paycheck, and they also packed me food to go home with. And they also noticed that I had anger problems and they talked to me and were concerned about my well-being. And I also had another thing, I was homeless, living outside or walking around late at night, or sleeping on a person's chair, and I told them I don't sleep.

They said you can come home with us and they made me feel like their own son. Even the co-workers reached out to me when I had to be admitted to a hospital for all types of stuff. But I'm still working and I get tips and people have asked me to dance and teach them dance moves. I love being a waver!!! I thank God for blessing me with this job, and I will never forget how they helped me out and made me feel like a brand new person.

Out of My Comfort Zone

By Liza Kearns/Waver - Chesapeake, VA

I always wondered about the stories behind the wavers. I finally decided to apply this year and give it a try. My story is unique. If you knew me you'd never expect me to be in this position, but I decided to step out of my comfort zone and go for some adventure. I was surprised by what I learned on the journey and felt inspired to tell my story in a blog: www.costumedmama.wordpress.com.

I would now describe myself as a fanatical waver. I have posted lots of pictures of me with my props and costume embellishments. Check it out.

It's the last week of tax season and I'm going to go out with a bang. Thanks for the experience, Liberty Tax!

The Difference a Smile Can Make

Larry Walsh/Zee - Bristol, RI

I have a young lady who works for me as a fanatical waver in my Bristol, RI office. Check out her Facebook post and I think you'll understand why I think she is employee # Awesome!

"I just want to take a moment to share something very touching that happened to me today while I was working at Liberty Tax. A man parked his car, got out, and approached me. I said hello and he proceeded to tell me about the positive impact I make on his days. He told me that each day he sees me, I always have on a smile, and when he's had a bad day at work it makes him feel better. I went to shake his hand and he stopped me to say that he wanted me to have a coffee on him and gave me a gift card to Dunkin Donuts. This was a very touching gesture and it is a moment I will never forget."

You can see her post at www.facebook.com/LTS12261

I Love Waving to People

Rebecca Raisman/Waver - Waukegan, IL

I love working at Liberty Tax and I'm a 4th year waver. In 2011, I was unemployed and was looking for a job, so I went to Liberty Tax in Waukegan, IL. I filled out an application and I did a tryout, and got the job just like that. I was so happy and excited to have something, after being unemployed for a while.

When I worked, I would put on the Statue of Liberty costume and I would go out and dance and wave. People would wave back and honk their horns. In 2012, I went to a different Liberty Tax and got to be a waver there. I had so much fun working for my boss - he treated everyone so well by providing snacks, giving a bonus at the end (of the season) and having a dinner party.

I love waving to people and putting smiles on their faces. People even come up to me to take a picture with them, and it just makes me feel good. I totally recommend Liberty Tax. The people are great to work with, friendly, and they work so hard during tax season. We have people come back year after year, and they say that they always look forward seeing a waver on the corner and getting their taxes done with Liberty Tax. When you provide great customer service and go above and beyond, you will have a customer for life. They will keep coming back year after year.

Jeremy's Message Has to Be Heard

Christian Smooth/Filmmaker - Annapolis, MD

Everyday I would see this guy dancing practically in the middle of the road. He would be out dancing no matter the condition rain or snow. I was interested to know why he danced and who he was as a person. It turned out I knew the guy.

I did not really recognize him because he had lost a lot of weight from his dancing. So I went out and interviewed him and he had nothing but positive things to say. Jeremy bought smiles to peoples faces in his Liberty costume. Filming him was only natural. Jeremy's message is positive and it has to be heard. Visit www.fanaticalatliberty.com to hear more of Jeremy's story!

The Opportunity to Work

By Jeneen Giannandrea/Zee - Dedham, MA

I am the franchise owner of the Liberty Tax in Dedham, MA. My story is regarding my wavers. I have changed the lives of some very special people by giving them the opportunity to work. In turn, they have changed my life. I merely am giving them the chance they deserve to work and to be part of something. The Neponset River House is a service of Riverside Community Care, a non-profit organization that provides mental health care, developmental and cognitive disability services, substance abuse treatment and other human services in over 50 Massachusetts cities and towns.

I have been so impressed with my staff of wavers and their work ethic and their gratitude for giving them a chance. "Thank you for being nice to me and giving me a chance," is a text I got from one of my wavers, John Harrop. Every single person I have employed from the Riverside House has reached out to me and thanked me for merely giving them a chance.

It has been my pleasure employing members of the Neponset River House and giving these very worthy people a chance to work. In 2013, I was honored at the Massachusetts State House with a community service award that I was very proud to accept.

Blessing in Disguise

By Timmithy Longoria/Waver and Marketing - Grande Prairie, TX

I'm Timmithy Longoria and this is my Liberty story. In order to understand my story and why Liberty means so much to me, you have to know my past. Starting off in life, I came from a broken home and an unstable life. I was a runaway at the age of 14 from an abusive home that did not accept me as being transgender, and thereafter the path my life was on, was not a good one. My actions and irresponsible mistakes finally caught up to me. I found myself in jail and going through the justice system. I was homeless and devastated, but little did I know this was a blessing in disguise.

In 2012, when I was finally done with the justice system, I made the choice to move forward in a positive manner. I enrolled in college and now was in the market for employment. I knew securing employment would not be easy, but little did I know it would be harder than I had thought.

Applying for many jobs and explaining my gap in employment and my now criminal background, almost all of my prospective employers, would not give me a chance. I did not feel sorry for myself, because I knew that this was a consequence of my mistakes, but I did begin to become discouraged. I felt as if my educational background and previous employment history was erased by the stigma of having a criminal background.

One day, I was walking home from putting in applications to nearby establishments, when I saw a Liberty Tax waver holding a sign, "Now hiring." I decided to take a chance, and I spoke to the manager and filled out an application. The manager, Mrs. Michelle, asked me if I would like to audition to be a waver. I said "yes." My chance finally came; someone decided to give me the opportunity to work and prove my worth despite my past mistakes, and having a non-traditional sexual identity. I was now employed. At first, I had my doubts and was nervous about being a waver, it seemed so menial, but the people at Liberty Tax treated me with respect and dignity. I was as much a part of the Liberty family as everyone.

I have been working for Liberty for two seasons, and plan to keep coming back. The people here at Liberty have become friends and family to me. I have had many opportunities allotted to me. While working for Liberty, I have worked as a waver and still do. I have done marketing, helped around the office, and next season I plan on taking the classes and working as a preparer. Liberty has helped me gain a sense of pride, a steady employment history, employment skills and a great and positive support system. Liberty Tax has truly touched and changed my life for the better.

Finishing Strong

Wayne Carlson/Waver, then Tax Preparer - Hutchinson, MN

In fall of 2010, my parents started doing a lot of rumbling about starting up a new business and they told me there would be a job opportunity. Well, being that I had been unemployed and living with them since 2008, I was excited to see what I would be doing. I was a sign waver. Due to the fact that we are in Hutchinson, Minnesota the first part of the season was quite cold, but I did not quit and finished the season off. Tax season 2013, my parents decided I should be a tax preparer, which is not a bad job.

I completed tax school, and all the rest of that fairly easily and we had a very good season. Well, here is where my parents starting this business started changing my life. I landed a job at Menards in less than 24 hours of applying as a morning stock. The reason being it had to do with me being able to state clearly I had been successful in a detail oriented job, and being able to show that I had a clear path of advancement from the previous year.

So, as it stands right now I have rehabbed my student loans and am looking at going back to college, still debating for what program or major. However, given that my parents own Liberty Tax and as part of that business, they do bookkeeping on the side - accounting is looking good for something I might decide to go into.

As tax season 2014 is looking to finish strong, and I can say beyond a shadow of a doubt, had my parents not taken the risk on Liberty, that I would probably still be living in their basement playing video games with no prospect of going back to college, nor of having the beautiful girlfriend who graced my life shortly before tax season 2014.

A Marriage Made in Liberty

By Becky Elder/Zee and Area Developer - Albany, GA

Our first tax season, a young man came into the office to apply for the waver position. He was very polite, mannerly, upfront and honest. Because of this great first impression, I took him into the break room and gave him an immediate interview. He told me that he was looking for an "honest job." He went on to tell me about some past gang activity that led to incarceration. He wanted to change his life for the better. Because I respected his upfront and honest approach, I called his references, let him audition, and offered him the waver position. His girlfriend was with him and she wanted to audition also. They both worked as wavers our first tax season.

Mid-way through the tax season, Jason and Shardae got married. They excelled in the waver position. Jason would watch YouTube waver videos on his own time and then took the initiative to train other wavers. He did this without being told to. I was thrilled with their self-motivation and pride that they took to spread the Liberty culture to others.

Jason and Shardae are beginning their third season with Liberty Tax in Albany, Georgia. They were promoted to waver trainers and managers in their second tax season. They are responsible for taking applications, coordinating auditions, hiring, training and scheduling wavers for all locations. They are a tremendous asset to our organization and its success. They are expecting their first child in May, 2014. Yes, they even planned their family around tax season!

Everyone Deserves a Chance

By Brian Scott/Zee - Northern VA

I have a waver who has been with me for the past three tax seasons. He saw an ad I ran for wavers in the paper, and called for an interview. When he came in, I showed him the training video and took him out to see what he could do. He was full of energy, but at the same time you could tell he had been down on his luck for a while. After the tryout, I offered him a job and he was very appreciative.

The next thing surprised me the most. He asked if he could speak with me outside. He told me that he really needed the job, but wanted to be honest with me since I had been so nice to him. He told me that he had a criminal record and, because of this, no one was willing to give him a chance at any job. He then proceeded to tell me that he would understand if I didn't want to hire him either. I asked him if he would be a good worker, to which he said emphatically, "Yes!" I told him that he had paid his debt to society and deserved a chance. He is an excellent waver, one of the very best I have seen!

The best part of the story is that I was able to provide him with a reference letter for his job application at Chick-Fil-A, where he has been employed now for a couple of years. He has become a valued employee there. He keeps coming back, he says, because he enjoys making people smile and because Liberty helped get him back on his feet, and was willing to give him a chance when no one else would.

MATTERS

FAMILY MATTERS

Liberty Tax and the Olympics?

By Linda Goepper/Zee - Lawrenceburg, IN
(Fanatical Award Winner and Olympic Mom!)

Liberty Tax and the Olympics? Our Liberty Tax business created an incredible platform for us to raise our family. We have four children, and they have all seen what it takes to build a business—risk, drive, creativity, hard work, and perseverance. They have all helped—they have participated in parades, cleaned the office, worked the festivals and helped with maintenance projects. They have seen the highs and the lows. They live with the philosophy of Set the Standard, Improve Each Day and Have Some Fun. We live this mission statement and have used this to help our kids understand how to attack life.

Nick, our oldest son, medaled in the Olympics this year. We have two daughters that are competitive gymnasts. Our youngest does a little bit of everything. Wow. How could this happen? Liberty Tax. We were able to create a unique schedule with our work and family to allow the kids to pursue their dreams. And, they learned how to do this, by modeling their parents and what we were able to teach them through our involvement with Liberty. They have worked with us, they have attended conventions, and they have created relationships with employees –learning about all different types of people.

Nick has handled the media in a relaxed and mature way. Kasey (age 17) coordinated a lot of the media and post-Olympic events. Bradee tackled her fear of cameras and interviews, and Jason learned to communicate with the Russians and to lead us to our destinations. They have always been part of the Liberty Tax world and they have been able to take their experience with our business and apply it to great life adventures. Nick has worked hard. He has set goals. He has fallen down and learned to get right back up. He knows that creativity sets you apart. He knows you have to be fanatical about what you do in order to be successful. Nick's ski flew off during a competition and he just landed on one ski and kept going. Nick motivates me---and I am his mom, how crazy is that?

---

19 February 2014

By Bob and Carolyn Grace/Zees - Danville, VA

March 13, 2013, Temika Chaney, a tax preparer since 2008, informed Carolyn and I that she had been diagnosed with breast cancer. She had a mastectomy during the next couple of months. Her extended care was composed of chemo and radiation therapy. I was in the office during November 2013, when she called and asked if I could do some notary work for her to which I responded, "of course."

The documents that she wanted notarized were a living will and her Last Will and Testament. Carolyn came in before I had finished and Temika told us that the cancer had spread to her liver and bones. She said that she was making preparations for death.

Carolyn indicated that she should have a good Christmas with her children (two boys, ages 2 and nine). She said that her boys would just have to understand that she had spent all of her money on medication. Carolyn asked what her boys needed and wanted. Armed with this information, her Liberty family had a Temika Christmas party on December 19 that involved all of our preparers and marketing employees.

There were more gifts for Temika and her boys than would fit in her car trunk. Her children caught her bringing in the gifts. There was also a substantial monetary gift for her, in case we missed something. She said that it was one the best Christmas days of her recent time. Temika passed today at 3am. It is gratifying that her small family could have some pleasant memory of her last days.

My Grandma's Last Hour

By Jamie Massaro/Business Analyst,
Libtax Software - Corporate Headquarters

I'm originally from Michigan, so most of my immediate family still lives there. I started working at Liberty in June of 2011. On February 1, 2012, my grandmother in Michigan, who I have always been closer to than just about anyone, was diagnosed with stage 4 lung cancer. It was devastating to me not only that she got the diagnosis, but that I was so far away and couldn't spend more time with her and help take care of her through her treatments.

I talked about the situation with my managers, and they reminded me that family comes first and told me to do what I needed to do to take care of things and not worry so much about work. Because of this, I was able to spend about a week out of a month, for several months, in Michigan taking care of her, and logging into work remotely when needed – but even then, my team jumped in and covered a great deal of my work without me ever asking. I was able to spend a lot of time with my grandma. In January of 2013, her health rapidly declined, and even though we had software releases going out in preparation for tax season, my managers didn't hesitate to let me go spend time with her. It was the last full week I ever got to spend with her. A couple weeks later, I got a call that she had hours left. Once more, I was told to do what I needed to do, and I was able to catch a flight out to Michigan and managed to spend my grandma's last hour alive with her and my immediate family.

I've never had a job before that's allowed me to spend this much time with my family, and I think that even if I had still lived in Michigan, I probably wouldn't have been able to both keep a job and spend that amount of quality time with my grandmother in her last year. That time with her has been the most valuable thing I could have ever had. I simply cannot express in words just how grateful I am to have had it, and the peace of mind that came with knowing I didn't have to worry about losing a job and trying to still afford to pay bills. Because of this, I really don't have any regrets at all with how my last year with her went, and I have some memories that will last for the rest of my life. Liberty's value of placing family first has meant more to me than anything.

On top of all that, I've met some amazing people through working here that have become like family to me. I have gained so much knowledge and job experience that I'm at a place I couldn't have imagined I would be in a few years ago. The tuition reimbursement plan has allowed me to go back to school, which is also helping me change my life for the better. I have no idea where I'd be right now if I wasn't here, and I appreciate all the opportunities I have every single day.

Corporate Attorney AND Mom

By Kathleen Curry/Corporate Counsel - Liberty Corporate

John Hewitt has had a huge influence on my life. An interview with John led me to accept a corporate counsel position with Jackson Hewitt immediately upon graduating from law school in 1992. Thanks to John, I had the opportunity to perform as a business partner in a dynamic tax organization rather than working as a nameless, faceless junior attorney within a law firm. A few months after joining Jackson Hewitt, John asked me to manage the Legal Department. Jackson Hewitt was expanding rapidly at this time, with the expected bumps and hurdles. John juggled countless issues and expected his managers to do the same. Employees from various departments worked together, pitching in as necessary to get the job done.

At one point, John asked that I manage the Tax and Software Department, in addition to the Legal Department. This challenge highlighted my need to learn to delegate and to focus on priorities. John's advice was "First things first, second things - not at all." That advice, and the associated skills that I eventually learned, have been invaluable. At another point in my career at Jackson Hewitt, I was called upon to act as the regional director for all new franchisees, while also managing the Training Department. I can still remember the day that John told me "If you aren't monitoring it, it isn't happening." That was such frustrating advice at the time, and now I can't count the number of times that I have used and repeated that advice over the years. After John left Jackson Hewitt, I remained at the company to complete the tax season as the Regional Director for new franchisees. I remember sitting with my supervisor as he tried to figure out how to provide daily performance projections for franchisees. Previously, John had managed this process and the franchisees had come to depend on the projections for staffing and cash flow purposes. Without John, the projections were really just uneducated guesswork. What a mess.

When John decided to form a new, improved tax company, I jumped at the chance to be a part of the opportunity. I truly believed, and still believe, that John would make a success of any venture in which he invested his time, energy, and leadership capabilities. The beginning of Liberty Tax Service was an exciting time. Each day held uncertainty, but the uncertainty was filled with promise. The company headquarters consisted of a very small office space with two offices. John shared a desk, not just an office, with Jack Seal. Martha, Donna, and I shared another office. Jeff Sharp, our IT Department, couldn't have an office because there was no space for an office for him. However, it soon became apparent that office space didn't matter much because we would be spending so much time in Winnipeg. John didn't exempt himself from the week-long trips to Winnipeg that all managers (and everyone was a manager) enjoyed during tax season. In my experience, John has never been a suit who sits in the corner office telling others what to do. John is ready, willing and able to contribute personally. As the years have gone by, my interaction with John has become infrequent. I choose to believe that this is because John has come to trust my judgment and not just because he is juggling even more issues. However, to this day, as I address various decision points during my workday, I consider the advice that I have learned from John Hewitt.

During this period of challenging and truly fun work experience with Jackson Hewitt and Liberty Tax Service, I married a wonderful man. Soon thereafter, we were blessed with two fabulous children. And, I am humbled to say that John Hewitt stepped in again to make my life even more amazing. John has allowed me to work from home three days a week. This flexible schedule has allowed me to enjoy my children and my husband. Thanks to John, I have been a part of their daily lives: from diapers to preschool to forgotten lunches to homework review to daily sports practices. I may have missed a hit or two due to my taking a conference call during a practice or even a game. My house is not as clean as it should be because I feel compelled to answer email as quickly as possible. But, thanks to John Hewitt, I have been able to perform as a business partner and as a mom. As I look back over the past (don't make me count) number of years, I most appreciate John Hewitt for his allowing me to be a corporate attorney AND mom. Thank you, John.

I am Changed Forever

By Demetrius Thomas/Receptionist,
Customer Service Representative - Liberty Corporate

After we closed our business, I was unemployed for about two years before I joined Liberty. Not only did Liberty change my life by giving me a job and security, they gave me the opportunity to better myself professionally. Liberty offered me training outside of my immediate job, and just watching Liberty Tax Service grow has been a valuable lesson in enterprise. The work environment is encouraging and the overall culture is unparalleled by any organization I have been a part of before. Liberty really gives a lot to their employees and makes sure they are comfortable and enjoy themselves, while also achieving company goals.

I have seen the opportunity for advancement and longevity through many employees who have been with Liberty for a long time, some from the very beginning. This was the first job (besides running my own business) where I was excited about the prospect of staying for more than a year, and here it is, three years later. I feel more stable and at home in my work, which definitely makes my personal life just that much easier to deal with. I know that I can advance in my current department, move to another or one day open up a Liberty Tax Service franchise where I can run my own business and still be a part of an organization I have come to love.

I also know that if I leave, I leave a more skilled and knowledgeable person and I will take with me the practices and values learned at Liberty to enhance wherever I land. I am changed forever and am thankful to be a part of Liberty Tax Service.

Work Hard, Get Recognized, Get Rewarded

By Synclair Thomas/Lead Receptionist/Customer Service Representative - Liberty Corporate

In November 2008, I lost my two retail stores, had a pregnant girlfriend, and was evicted from my apartment, where my mother, two brothers, said girlfriend and a close friend of mine all stayed with me. I hadn't been able to keep up with bills and rent because the recession was in full swing and it had been tough enough trying to keep my stores afloat, let alone paying my own stuff. I had been managing these stores basically since getting out of high school, and foolishly thought I'd ride that out for a long while.

Desperate and with no income, I hit the job hunt trail, like a lot of folks during that dark period. A friend of mine informed me that her department at Liberty Tax Service, corporate office was hiring. I didn't even know Liberty's corporate office was IN Virginia. I interviewed and got hired at a time I needed it the most.

Now, you may say "Well, ANYONE who needed workers could have hired you," and that's a fair assessment. It's what Liberty did for me AFTER being hired that matters. I was supposed to be seasonal, but I worked my tail off and was kept on after tax season. That became a constant theme: work hard, get recognized for that hard work, get rewarded. Did I mention 'have fun in between'?

This company works super hard and plays just as hard (if not a bit harder - ha ha) and that kind of atmosphere is ideal for a guy like me who used to work for myself. I've now been here for five years and this is my sixth tax season. It's also a family environment that encourages us to bring our closest companions into the fold. I've gotten jobs for my twin brother, my daughter's mother, and my sister-in-law during my tenure here. I've been sent to various trainings to further my career and hone my craft. I've also had the great pleasure of meeting a group of folks who I might not have had such close relationships with outside of here. I'm thrilled to be a part of a company such as this one, and am glad to do my part to get us to that 2020 goal of becoming the largest, greatest tax company in the universe.

Baby Announcement - Maria Lucia Artese (7lbs, 13oz)

By Rich Artese/VP and CIO of Technology - Liberty Corporate
(the day after Maria's birth)

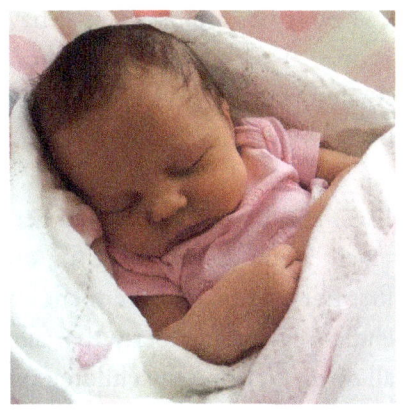

I have to tell you. I've worked in a lot of large companies, and have been in much more senior positions than my job at Liberty, but I have never received the number of congratulations or well wishes on any life event as I have from my Liberty family. My wife's room is adorned with flower arrangements from Ops and Technology and JTH Financial and several individuals. It is such a blessing to be surrounded by such positive people who care. I even received emails from some staffers that only know me by passing by in the hallway.

Anytime anyone questions the kind of culture John has built at LTS, feel free to send them to me. I'm not the most tenured employee, but I really do feel like I am part of a very special group of people.

Before Liberty, I Was Giving Up Hope

By Lisa Lewis/Mapping Analyst - Liberty Corporate

My name is Lisa Lewis and I'm a mapping analyst at Liberty Corporate. I have two boys, ages six and ten. Most of their lives, I have spent running pizza shops or as a delivery driver. Most of their lives, they have spent with babysitters. I hadn't been back to Illinois, where my family lives, for six years. My father had a heart attack and I did not have the money or opportunity to go see him. I'm only one person and now I know that the life-changing impact of Liberty Tax is very personal.

I'm in a work-study program at Bryant and Stratton College, and my boss suggested that I apply to Liberty. I almost had a panic attack thinking about doing somebody's taxes. Coming from running a pizza shop, I was unaware of all the levels of people in Liberty to support each other. In a pizza shop, there is only one level - you. You do everything from advertising, employee management, customer service, controlling costs, fixing anything that breaks, etc.

I originally started in the call center last January, and I loved working for Liberty so much that I started to get sad when March came around and I knew it was almost over. I have never met a more supportive group of people. I took a chance, without expecting a response, for the Mapping Analyst position and to my surprise I was chosen. Since that time, it has been a whole new world for me.

When my children are sick, I no longer panic about whether or not I will still have a job, if I go get them. My kids and I get to spend time together and actually have fun on the weekends. This Easter will mark the first full year that I have spent every holiday with my children. There are endless events at Liberty that allow me to have a little time out, and that allow me to bring my children out and enjoy time with them.

I now have medical and dental benefits for us. I have a paid vacation so I will finally get the opportunity to go home and see my family who I miss very much. In addition, I am a college student who is half way through my bachelor's degree. Before Liberty, I was giving up hope of completing school, because I did not have the funding. Now, not only does my schedule work perfectly so I can take the classes I need, my bosses are researching tuition reimbursement to help me finish my degree. Any help is one step closer.

In addition to all of this, Liberty offers classes to help me become a better employee. There are opportunities available, if I work hard enough, to help me become self-sufficient and someone my children can be proud of. Hopefully, I can convince them to start their careers at Liberty when the time comes. I know that I'm not out here changing the world yet, but with a corporation like Liberty, I have all the right people directing me.

For the first time, I have everything I could ever want and need, and Liberty Tax made it all possible. Thank you for everything, Liberty!

P.S. I was given a gift certificate to Great Wolf Lodge, randomly, at my desk during Christmas. It was signed Secret Santa Sister. That's why I have that picture. It was the nicest thing anybody has done for me, and I still don't know who Secret Santa Sister is.

Stop and Listen

Joan Hughes/Tax Preparer - Irmo, SC

Our story began several years ago, when Danny (my husband) was diagnosed with Renal Failure. Over each passing year, his kidney functions have decreased to the point where he is currently at 13% function, which means a kidney transplant is required within the next year or so. We began the process of being tested last August for Danny to be placed on the transplant list and he has been approved at GRU (Georgia Regents Univ.) in Augusta, Georgia (formerly MCG) and now we have testing at MUSC (Medical Univ. of SC) in Charleston and Carolina Medical Center in Charlotte, NC after tax season is over.

What I would like to share is that when you think you are all alone in this world and you are wrapped up in your problems, stop and listen. Danny had a customer who is on the heart transplant list. I have had a customer who is also on the kidney transplant list at GRU, but I was able to educate her about she needs to be on MUSC and CMC's list as well. (Per the guidelines you can be on up to 3 lists, but must live within 5 hours of the medical facility and she did not know this).

When you attend the orientations about being placed on the kidney transplant list, each orientation is different and the facilitators may leave out information or may think it something that you already know. It was very rewarding knowing that not only I was able to help this couple complete their taxes, but maybe was able to give her a new lease on life by sharing what Danny is going through and what we have learned about kidney transplant. Also, I took the paperwork for a drop off return and just in talking with Mrs. Thomas (because of the size of the box with medical and pharmacy receipts) I discovered that her husband had a kidney transplant in December of 2013 at GRU and that his caseworker is Lynn, who is also Danny's.

It is sad that Danny is going through this, but through our jobs this season at Liberty we have learned that we are not alone. Plus not only have we made a difference in helping prepare different individuals taxes, maybe we have made a difference in someone receiving a kidney faster by educating her on the importance of being listed at as many medical facilities as possible. Even though it is a national donor registry, they try to keep the organs local and sometimes it is easier to use locally, because there is a 24-hour time frame.

This story may not seem important to anyone but to know that we are not in this boat alone, and that we were able to share our knowledge of the kidney transplant protocol has been wonderful. If Danny had not been employed by Mr. Larry last year and recruited me this year, we would not have been able to share this and possibly make a difference in this young mother's life and/or quality of life. This means the world to us that we are able to take a negative and turn it into a positive.

Time with My Son

Dorothea Calhoun/Waver, Preparer - Phoenix, AZ

In 2011, I was a waver. Now I am a preparer on my second year. Having this job has given me the time that I wanted with my son. I work for Liberty from January until April, which is perfect because my son is in school during these months and I am off for the summer, so that we can do things as a family. Because this is a seasonal job, I can take my vacations during the summer to fun and exciting places with my son, without worrying about how it will affect us money-wise. I so enjoy working for this company and I plan to as long as I am able.

Gaining a New Family

By Michele Westbrook/Customer and Tax Preparer - Stedman, NC

I guess it all started last tax season when my husband and I went into Liberty to have our taxes filed and from the second we walked through the door, we were welcomed with big smiles and a very relaxing experience. I had been a stay-at-home mom for almost six years and was struggling to find work. My husband had been working seven days a week to take care of our growing family. I was almost at my wits end from so many dead ends until October of 2013; we received a phone call from Mrs. Donna Jackson. She had called to ask me if I was interested in learning about Liberty's Tax School.

I attended the three-month tax classes and the Rapid Class before tax season began and by the time the "school" was over I felt like I was gaining a new family instead of an employer. Mrs. Gail Flowers and Mrs. Donna Jackson are two of the kindest and most down to earth people I have ever met and they have a way of making everyone that comes into our store feel like they are at home. Our little group of ladies that work together really go out their way to help each other grow and learn, and I thank God everyday for bringing Liberty into my life.

Liberty has been a true blessing to my family in our time of need, and I am proud to say that I am a part of the Liberty family!

My Daughter's Guardian Angel

By Shannon Bird/General Manager - Yakima, WA

In August of 2012, I ran an ad for our Tax Class. A young Hispanic woman (I'll call her Lilith) answered the ad. She went through the class with many other people, and I noticed that, although English wasn't her first language and she struggled, she was very hard working and tenacious.

One day Lilith came to me, shortly after the class had ended, and told me she really needed to work right away. She broke down crying, saying her husband had "done something stupid." Rather than be arrested and pay for it, he had run off to Mexico, leaving her and two babies behind. She had no income and was going to be evicted. In the Hispanic community, family is everything and Lilith had none here in the states. She was so bereft! I gave her a big hug and assured her everything would be okay, then we talked about what she should do next. She didn't want to go back to Mexico after she had worked so hard to become a citizen here.

I gave her a job right away as our receptionist until she could get through with her certification test and get her PTIN. Some days she had to bring the babies to work with her because she had no one to care for them. I helped her file her back tax returns for free, then paid for her PTIN. Again, she broke down in tears, saying I had no idea what this meant to her for me to help her.

Lilith became one of our tax preparers for a short while, earning enough money to see her through the roughest part. Then, one day she came into the office looking very sad. She had received a job offer for full-time, year-round, steady work at one of the area packinghouses and although she didn't want to leave us, she had no choice. Again she cried, thanking me for helping her, hugging me and calling me an angel for all I did, although I felt I only did what any human being would do. We were all so happy she had a way to work steadily to take care of herself and the children, and with benefits! Eventually, her parents came in from Mexico to help her.

During this tax season, she came in with her babies to file her return. The babies have become toddlers but felt completely at home in our little office. They must have some memories of being here before, when their mother needed a little help. It was so good to see her! And she brought her mother, who had come back to visit from Mexico. Meeting her for the first time, Lilith's mother grabbed my hand and smiled gently at me, and in her broken English she said, "Thank you for being my daughter's guardian angel."

Bringing Gizzy to Work With Me!

By Amanda Carter/Customer Service - Benton, TN

I started working at Liberty Tax 5 years ago, and even though it is only seasonal work, I will forever be a faithful employee. Adam and Betty Standridge are the franchise owners for my office. They are the most wonderful human beings I've ever met in my life, and by far the best bosses!

It is very rare that places of business will let you bring a pet with you to work, especially when it's the peak time of tax season. My wonderful bosses let me bring Gizzy to work with me. It was amazing - when I made the foam Liberty crown to fit his small head, he wore it around the office with a proud look on his face.

He would also sit on my desk and help me greet the clients. To everyone's amazement, Gizzy would walk up to the clients and they would pick him up and set him in their laps while they were in midst of filing their returns. A lot of clients thanked me for bringing him to work with me, and said that he helped relieve some of their stress, due to the overwhelming nature of tax time. It was a wonderful experience all together.

I love my son, Gizzy!

CHALLENGE OURSELVES,

CHALLENGE EACH OTHER,

BREAK BOUNDARIES

CHALLENGE OURSELVES, CHALLENGE EACH OTHER, BREAK BOUNDARIES

I am a Survivor

By Greg Carafello/Zee - 34 Stores

In 2001, I owned a digital printing company operating in the World Trade Center in New York. On September 11th, I lost my one of my best friends, watched my business begin to crumble, but never lost my faith in the American dream.

I am a survivor of the terrorist attacks that changed our reality in this country. For two years, I struggled to rebuild my $4 million business but by 2003, revenues dropped to $600,000 and we had to close our doors.

Tragedy taught me that you only go around once in life, and we can't be afraid to take a chance. We did that by investing in two franchise systems: Cartridge World (70 stores) and Liberty (34 stores). While all of us survivors have stories of 9/11, this story is about the difference Liberty has made in my life, and why the Liberty system isn't like any other I've experienced.

First of all, Liberty is unique because of the CEO, John Hewitt. He is personally engaged with his franchisees, teaching leadership with a laser-like focus. You can't put a price on how valuable that is. He genuinely shows caring and concern, and has created many millionaires through his system.

Secondly, he understands both the corporate culture and entrepreneurial mind. I've never seen anything like it. If you want an education that's equivalent to a Harvard MBA, you want to learn from a true winner. You don't realize how important passion and expertise is until you don't have it.

Finally, John knows how to help others set and achieve their goals. He knows how to start a business, finance it, and drive it forward everyday. Being a survivor is about picking yourself up when you fall, or tragedy strikes. If you are hoping to partner with a true winner, in my experience, John is my choice and Liberty is my system.

---

51 Stores and Counting!

By Bablu Shahabuddin/Top Zee and Area Developer

Liberty has changed my life dramatically. I'm financially independent, and I now know what I'm doing. Liberty's proven system gave me the opportunity to live up to my potential, and live my dream. I always dreamed of taking control of my business life, but Liberty made it possible. To be a winner, you have to really love what you do. I hate to lose. My father always told me that you have to enjoy winning and I do. If I lose, I go crazy. I lose sleep!

When I joined Liberty, I had saved up $30,000, I borrowed $20,000 from my mother, and I opened two offices. Beginning the businesses needed more than that – all the supplies, signage, everything else – I maxed out my credit cards to get those. We did well, about $175,000 in revenue, which was okay.

Since then, we've been growing. In New York, I have 32 stores, 2 in New Jersey, 4 in Westchester County, one in Massachusetts, 5 in Las Vegas, and 7 in Los Angeles. That's 51 stores and counting.

Everybody dreams, but I didn't know if it was possible. The system that John Hewitt has put in place made the difference. He tells you what needs to be done and when it needs to be done. Timing is very important – if you do things at the right time, then you become successful. The Liberty system tells you what needs to be accomplished each day.

Financially, John helped us expand by providing financing. Most importantly, he believed in me. When I told him I wanted 50-60 offices, he believed it. As a newcomer, if you go to the bank and tell them that you want to expand that much (and I need a million dollars!), they would laugh at me.

John gave me his support, and that made me very successful.

From Homemaker to Business Owner

By Margaret Taylor/Zee - Virginia Beach, VA

I was a stay-at-home mom for 18 years and I didn't have any business experience. My husband worked for John Hewitt and encouraged me to take the 5-day Rapid Class to learn tax preparation. I remember feeling scared, thinking I don't want to go! Here I was, sitting in this class with maybe 15 other people and everybody was clicking away at the computer. I was just sitting there and sitting there, doing nothing. My instructor wondered what was going on with me. Here's the truth - I didn't know how to turn a computer on. That's how little I knew. Seriously! I went from homemaker to business owner: a franchisee, now with three stores, and I'm considering becoming an area developer.

This didn't happen overnight. First, I worked for another franchisee in the back office, but I loved the Liberty business model. I realized that for the right person, this could be life changing. That turned out to be me.

The best part of the business is the spirit of philanthropy. John Hewitt is a person of integrity: giving and forgiving. Plus, I still get to be a mom, this time to many of my young team members. For example, I brought on board, several years ago, a 16 year old waver, Jemell, (who is still actively working with me.) This was his first job. He works very hard, is extremely loyal, and happens to be an ABSOLUTELY GREAT WAVER. He has never made excuses for getting to work, subsequently riding his bike to work every shift. Last year, when tax season was over, after saving every penny of his earnings, he bought a car.

Or there is Kristen. I'll never forget Kristen, a single mom, who worked very hard to learn something new and challenging, become a tax professional, in order to grow and support her son. Our culture has also shaped the lives of so many college interns who, as a product of graduation, have to do a brief stint with us. Unbeknownst to them and me, that time had a long-term positive impact still to this day and many continue to stay in touch and call to thank us. We even had a mother/daughter waver team who were 60 and 80 years old respectively!

There's something about Liberty and these four walls that inspire hope and giving. For me, it's ALL about the little things. Remember, I didn't even know how to turn a computer on. If this stay-at-home mom can become a successful Liberty franchisee, anyone can.

John Saw What I Could Become

By Sandy Raiter/Tax Specialist - Liberty Headquarters

In 1976, I was a Navy wife, stay-at-home mother looking for an exciting job. I answered an ad for tax preparer training and fell in love with taxes. I worked for Mel Jackson until 1982, when John Hewitt bought the company. He brought many new ideas and changes. The one that I did not like was the use of a computer program. I was so against computers that I did not even want my husband to have one in the house.

I loved the idea that a tax return was like a puzzle and I was the one in control of the pieces. I'm also a bit of a control freak, so I said I would not be using the computer but would continue to hand-write all the returns I did. John graciously allowed me to do this for about seven years. At one point in those years, I asked him if I would continue to have a job if I did not use the computer, and he said I would always have a job.

I was against using a computer, but I am not stupid. I could see the "handwriting on the wall," and with electronic filing I knew that my hand-written days were numbered. So I jumped into using the computer and the wonderful computer program that John had developed. As I used it, I realized that I did still have some control, but the computer remembered everything and made me a better tax preparer. Some years later, I also debugged the program. John said if I could use the system, then anyone could use it.

I have a degree in education but had never really used it. When I came to Liberty, John said he had an idea for training called Tax Academy. He let me design the curriculum and teach some of the courses. Without his wonderful way of seeing the whole person and analyzing their abilities, I would not be somewhat "computer literate," now able to do many things on the computer, and enjoying my senior years doing a job I love. John looks at what people can become, not what they are now. That's a great trait to have and that is why he will always be a person to admire.

Reach For Your Dreams

By Nancy Nelson/ Executive Assistant to the CEO
and Area Developer - Liberty Corporate

When I came to work for John Hewitt in 1995 at Jackson Hewitt, I thought I was there for the long haul. Within a short period, John had left the company and it was very apparent that the "suits" had taken over the company after he left. The culture totally changed, and not for the better!

I was delighted when John approached me to come work for his new and exciting venture, Liberty Tax Service. I joined the Liberty team in January 2000 and spent the next 14 years as a part of this growing, dynamic organization.

One thing I have learned is that when John suggests a new venture, he has put a lot of thought into his recommendation. In 2007, John asked Amy Wehrkamp and me if we had ever considered becoming Area Developers. I had been a part of the training team and was familiar with the operations aspect, while Amy had been a very successful franchise development rep. This seemed like a logical and doable partnership, so we took the AD plunge. At John's suggestion, we purchased the Tyler/Longview, TX, DMA (designated market area). Although this was a lot of debt for us to take on, Amy and I felt confident that John would not steer us wrong if we were willing to put in the hard work and dedication it requires to be successful.

Seven years later, we have helped the franchisees we support to become more and more successful, but we have also developed friendships with all of them. It gives us great pride to help them achieve business and life goals and dreams, and this experience would never have been possible without the support of John Hewitt.

Liberty Belles

Sandra Sutton/Office Manager - Houston, TX

My Liberty story is about my co-worker Jackie Chapman and how she has touched my life. I first met Jackie in my 2011, ten-week Basic Tax Class. She was unable to work with us that tax season because she was needed at home. But she returned that fall to retake the class and work the tax season, starting in January of 2013. She stayed in touch during the off-season by coming in and working on practice problems. In November, she discovered a lump in her breast and was diagnosed with triple-negative breast cancer, a rare and aggressive cancer.

She underwent a double mastectomy on December 20, 2013. Three weeks after surgery, Jackie was placed on the schedule to be the nighttime Lead Tax Preparer. She started chemotherapy the morning of February 26, and came to work as scheduled at 3pm that afternoon.

Jackie has now had five treatments and has not been late or missed a day of work because of these treatments. She had long hair but cut it short to prepare for the loss of her hair, and has now lost her hair. She has been an encourager to all of us at the office. She will not let us pity her or pamper her. To show our support we had pink polo style shirts made with the breast cancer ribbon on it and have nicknamed all of us "Liberty Belles."

A Marine Finds Liberty

By Eddie Thompson/Large Entity Support - Liberty Corporate

Leaving the United States Marine Corps, I knew I would never find the same work environment from which I had just left after 20 years. I retired from what I consider my second family. In the Corps, you worked hard, played hard, and made friends for a lifetime.

Shortly after returning to Virginia, my outlook was positive for finding work, but reality soon kicked in. First, I worked for a call center where the stress level was high, but the support from management was low. Everything felt automated and lifeless. Then I took another job for minimum wage, all while attending college to further my education.

One day, out of the blue, I received a call for a technical support job. I said "yes" and got it without even an interview because of my previous experience. I worried it was going to be another drone style job. But then I showed up for training at Liberty Tax Corporate Headquarters. The work was satisfying and restored my hope for the work field. I worked for five months until tax season ended.

In the off-season, I once again became unemployed. As soon I could, I sent my resume to Liberty Tax for the next season. I applied for a coach job hoping to help techs learn everything I did the year before. But because I did not have the flexibility due to school, I was asked to come back as a tech later in the year. I agreed. One Friday, I got a call from Sunny Haynes asking if I could start work a week early. I had known one of the coaches quit for a different job, and figured it was the job I applied for. However, when I arrived I was put in Large Entity Support. Here I get to work independently, helping people set up their offices for the tax season. I continue to learn more about my field while working with people who have great personalities and a great work ethic.

To add to my experience, shortly after I returned to Liberty Tax, my wife had our fourth child and I had to take some time off because of complications. I worried that since I was taking so much time off so soon after being hired, I would be out of work again. But I was given the time I needed to take care of family and flexible hours to complete my work.

I feel at home again, just like I did in the Marine Corps.

Life Changing

By Jack Seal/Zee and Former VP of Finance - Virginia Beach, VA

I learned more from John about business management, people management and human relations than I ever did in MBA school and in my Fortune 50 corporate career. Life changing, for me, was not so much about making money (although that sure helps!) but more about what I learned from John that changed my life personally. I'm grateful to have taken the journey with John from Jackson Hewitt days in 1989 through the present days with Liberty. I've enjoyed every minute and done it with pride.

Many of my life changing experiences occurred during my time working for John at Jackson Hewitt where I was in charge of operations. John personally worked with me to help me develop and understand management traits as well as to recognize and improve upon my strengths and weaknesses. I remember one instance where I had made a decision about an employee and John sat me down and said that I had made the wrong decision. I spent all day trying to convince John that I was right and the basis for the decision was based on sound thinking. John, as John does, listened to me but continued to say, "Nope—bad decision… for this reason." I left for the day determined to find a way to get him to understand and agree with me. Instead what happened for me was an "aha" moment when I realized the problem was not John, but it was about my ability to admit to myself that I'm not perfect and will make mistakes. John taught me that it's OK to make mistakes, just learn and grow from them. My outlook became that everything will not always be executed perfectly and excuses don't matter. There will always be mistakes, learn from them and improve. The lesson was empowering for me personally and I started to look at life's occurrences in a calmer and more positive light.

I have seen John give an opportunity to many people who started out as franchisees with essentially nothing except a great attitude and desire to succeed. If you work hard and are committed to success, John will give you a shot and provide you the resources to become successful. He's great at understanding what's inside of a person and wants to positively change the lives of as many people as he possibly can.

John is all about helping other people. One thing about John's desire to help others that really stands out to me is his passion to stop world hunger. He has committed a huge amount of time and resources for many years to this cause. John is not very interested in material things and is much more concerned with how he can positively change peoples' lives.

I'm truly grateful to have been associated with John for the past 25 years. I've always been amazed by John's strategic mind and his commitment to win and I have never seen his commitment waiver no matter the circumstances. I have always valued John's advice to me on both business and personal matters and have always felt that whenever he has given advice to me or anyone, it's been solely with that person's interests in mind.

Life changing for me is that hopefully some has rubbed off over the past 25 years.

Improve Each Day, Let Go of Yesterday

By Jean Field/Zee - Rock Hill, MO

I am a second year Zee. We definitely had a bumpy start our first season, but I was truly touched by several of the stories of my employees. I know God put me here in this part of Saint Louis for a reason. Saint Louis is known as the Gateway to the West, and all roads lead to Saint Louis. Our office is on the major bus route going west from the city. As a result many of my employees come to work by bus from all parts of the city. We are truly a diverse group of people.

One of my tax preparers, Aida G., took my Rapid Class last year as she wanted to understand her own situation better. Aida is always taking classes and learning something new, so she actually had no desire to be a preparer. Aida had been working as a server in ethnic restaurants where she didn't need to speak much. Aida is a native Russian speaker, with a college degree in chemistry, but has not had the confidence in her English skills to pursue better jobs. As result, she had been reluctant to even apply for jobs requiring her to communicate in English.

During the Rapid Class, it was obvious that Aida is very bright and her command of English was quite strong. With her kind demeanor and compassion for the less advantaged, she is a natural at the tax desk. By the end of last season, Aida had gained the confidence she needed in her ability to explain complex situations in English that she applied for a job at the local credit union as a teller, and is on her way! Most importantly, by gaining full time employment - with benefits - her husband was able to follow his passion as a chef. Working at Liberty has truly changed her life.

A little over half of my employees from last year have returned and, for each of them, joining Liberty has given them confidence in their abilities to take new life risks to improve their futures. For many, this is the first time someone has encouraged them to step outside of their comfort zone and supported their desire to better themselves.

I am constantly reminding myself to improve each day, and to let go of yesterday.

#1

Anonymous

It's amazing how the casual observance of such a simple number can have an unexpected and continued impact on your life. In one of my first meetings with John Hewitt, we were discussing our shared love of card playing. I'm not sure who challenged whom, but it wasn't long before we were engaged in a heated game of Spades.

The casual observance occurred when he wrote our names on the score pad. Although I was thrilled that he remembered my name, more importantly, I observed (and was intrigued) that instead of writing "John" on the score pad, he just simply put #1. I can't remember who won that first game, but I'm 99.9% sure it wasn't me.

That #1 theme continued throughout our relationship. His inspiration, wisdom, and guidance facilitated my success as a franchisee, helped me to form much better relationships, introduced me to new perspectives, and immensely raised my self-confidence. I've learned that advice from John is powerful beyond measure.

One interaction that particularly sticks out in my mind is when we were having a casual conversation and he asked me a simple question about my tax office. When I responded that I didn't know the answer he immediately retorted with "Well, who should I ask?" I don't know if he realized it at the time, but his question (although kind of funny) was extremely motivating. He was right – how was I going to be the #1 tax office in my territory if I couldn't answer such a simple question. My point is - and I'm sure there are thousands that can attest to this - is that a few words (or in my case a question) from John can be a catalyst for success.

The number one will always remind me of John's ambition, integrity, inspiration, tenaciousness, and generosity. It will always motivate me to strive for the best. My relationship with Liberty Tax Service and John Hewitt has unquestionably improved the quality of my life, and the quality of the lives of those I care about. And for that I thank you, #1.

Unlimited Opportunity

By Twaleetar Dale/Zee - Madison, AL

New Franchisee of Liberty. Liberty has taught me and educated me on how to truly be a business owner and not just work my business. The books we receive through the mail are great tools and I read each book. Liberty has forever changed the way I do things and think about life.

Liberty has allowed us to dream big and feel a lot better about finances. We are not where we want to be, but we are striving to get there.

Our store has not reached our personal goals, so we are planning to go to convention and talk to as many successful Zees we can. We are also going to visit to successful Zees' offices this summer and increase our marketing budget.

Thanks to Liberty, our family has an unlimited opportunity.

Enjoy the Journey

By Jim Davis/Liberty Tax Investor

John Hewitt and I have been friends for a long time. In many ways we are very different. John likes to be in the spotlight and I like the shadows. John likes to be around people most of the time and I like to stay to myself. But in at least one way, we're very much the same. We both have a strong sense of what should be done and will do it regardless of what other people think.

I've invested in two of John's companies. Both were privately held and investing in the stock was highly risky. I'm a conservative investor so what made me do it? Was it because of John's intelligence and experience in the tax industry? No, though he certainly has much of both. Was it because of his entrepreneurial spirit and his ability to turn an idea into a reality? Again, no. Was it because of his management style and his prescription for success? Once again, no. All these are important and John has these to a large extent. But other people also have these and investing with them may be a disaster. The reason I invested with John is that I knew he was totally honest. It's important to know that one thing you don't have to worry about is whether the owner is trying to do his best for the company and the stockholders. No matter how good your plans may be, they can go wrong. That's an unavoidable risk, but it's compounded if you can't be sure of the integrity of the owner. With John, this was never an issue.

One reason John is a success and has made a lot of money is that he doesn't care that much about making money. So why is he a success? Ultimately it's not because he follows certain formulas for success, but rather because he is who he is. Success is almost like a side effect. The goal he chose was to be the largest (actually I think he means best) tax company in the country. He has succeeded admirably so far towards that goal. But is the specific goal really that important? Would he not have succeeded at almost any goal he chose to pursue?

He built a successful tax business because he built it the way he thought it should be built. He didn't build it so that it would be a success. He imposed his vision of what a successful tax business should be, and a natural consequence is that it was a success. But success isn't the main goal; the causality doesn't run that way. You follow your vision and do what you think is right and success often follows. But the success isn't what really matters; the important thing is stamping reality in some part of the world with your vision. That's why John says, "Enjoy the journey."

Follow a Proven System

By Jesse Smith/Zee - North Carolina

I met Ray Dunn (Area Developer) at an IRS conference 10 years ago. Ray stayed in touch with me every year for the next 5 years, and finally asked me to listen in on one of John Hewitt's conference calls.

During the call, I was convinced that it would be easier to follow a proven system rather than continuing to create my own system. I had been a "mom and pop" tax business owner for more than 20 years. We now have 4 locations with Liberty, and will do more than 2,000 returns this year. We will add at least one location per year over the next 5 years. I am happy to be a part of Liberty, and I look forward to helping us reach number one by 2020.

It is Your Choice

Karen Redding/Zee - Fredericksburg, VA

At the onset of my franchise journey with Liberty Tax Service, my tax experience was limited to none. I am an accountant and loved working with numbers, but had absolutely no working experience or knowledge in retail tax preparation. I had always filed my own personal tax returns and I had taken another company's tax course out of curiosity ten years prior to joining Liberty. That was the limited knowledge I had to get started.

Ten years later, I teach and train new and existing tax preparers and audit many of the complicated tax returns prepared within my company. My personal franchises (I currently own three), prepare thousands of returns on an annual basis. I chose to personally use the resources provided to expand my knowledge of this industry, but have met many successful owners who have chosen to delegate that responsibility. The beauty of this relationship is that the necessary tools for your success are handed to you… and it is your choice as to how they can best be used in your organization!

It's My Time to Shine

By Hamida Chandrani/Zee – Los Angeles, CA

My name is Hamida Chandrani and this is my first year being a franchisee. I have always worked for someone until now and I have always helped them to be more successful and to get closer to achieving their dreams. My husband, Nazim Chandrani, started sweeping and mopping floors at his uncle's gas stations with minimum pay. He slowly started gaining experience behind the counter ringing up sales. In no time, the store revenue started going higher and higher due to his hard work, dedication, and outstanding customer service. His uncle gave him an opportunity to manage his stores, which lead to a partnership, and he then started taking ownership of those and many more stores.

My husband and I got an opportunity to be franchisees at Liberty Tax Service in August of 2013. I was tired of working for someone and helping them reach their dreams and the thought came into my mind, "IT'S MY TIME TO SHINE," and this is the moment that I turned my dreams into reality. We went for EOT (training) in September and moved from Georgia to Los Angeles in October. Leaving all my family and friends, we just did it. My husband and I closed the deal for 12 Liberty Tax stores in November. So far, this has been the most exciting adventure for me and I totally love it.

I feel the way Liberty Tax advertises the "Guerrilla Marketing" way is different, but it totally makes a difference and allows us to be on a more personal level with our workers and customers. We have been given the opportunity to meet, work, and help an array of different individuals. At the moment we are working with Morning Sky, a company that helps mentally challenged adults live their lives one day at a time. Right now we have three incredible marketers from the Morning Sky home. We will call people from the company every tax season because it is so rewarding to be able to help in the process of getting them involved back into the community. Waving, B2B and P2P (marketing), and even helping with our daily BBQ Weenie flipping.

It just gives us a great feeling of achievement and smile on our faces to be able to do something for our community.

Liberty Changed my Heart

By Bob Schneider/Franchise Development - Liberty Corporate

My heart caused me to lose almost everything, literally. After serving in the Marine Corp, I spent 27 years working in photography sales and had dozens of offices across the U.S. I helped the owners restructure and sometimes downsize. Yes, that meant firing people. In our first 28 years of marriage, we moved a lot and lived in 20 different homes.

My heart was always 100% in my work, until the day my heart decided to speed up and slow down at the same time, going wacko under this frantic pace. I underwent two lengthy heart surgeries. I'm lucky to be alive. I didn't realize at the time, that this was going to be the beginning of a new way of living. I couldn't work and lost everything. I started a small online business, but didn't know how we would survive or if we would ever be able to retire. That's when Jeff Dusza, my best friend, offered me a ground floor position as a Marketing Manager for a Liberty Tax store.

Fast-forward seven years....

I became a partner with Jeff, and eventually sold my share of the stores back to him. At a Christmas party, John Hewitt asked me if I wanted to buy a territory on my own. I said, "No way!" John spoke with my wife, Diane, about becoming a Zee. When I got back to the table, Diane announced that we were buying a store, becoming franchisees just days before Christmas. This announcement turned into a life-changing moment.

After the next tax season, we bought a second territory with five stores. The season after that, we then traded up to buy a small area development. Then once again, two years later, we traded up to partner on a much bigger area. Presently, I'm working on a third and fourth DMA. If this sounds confusing, just think of the game of Monopoly, trading up my green houses for red hotels.

A great seven years…

Financially, on paper, I went from losing everything to becoming a very successful businessman. Liberty has affected me in many ways. It's educated me on Corporate America and I've also learned more about the

NASDAQ than I ever could imagine. Liberty has helped me to help others, which is a love of mine. It's introduced me to some great friends and most importantly, has allowed my wife and me to be able to retire comfortably. Liberty will help my 6 grandchildren go to college, and will allow me to fish and golf when I want!

The best part is that I never have to stop helping people. I can retire from Liberty Corporate in 2020 and remain an Area Developer until I die. I will be able to assist Zees until my Alzheimer's kicks in! Who knew that heart surgery would result in my change of heart, in so many ways?

I Had Absolutely No Tax Knowledge

By Anthony Focca/Zee - Staten Island, NY

I was first told about Liberty Tax in 2008 by a co-worker. At the time, I had absolutely no tax knowledge but thought the company has a great concept and decided to take a shot. I purchased by first Liberty Tax Franchise that year and using the simple system, was able to have a successful first season.

Every year, I have opened another Liberty Tax office and I currently have six Liberty Tax Franchises in Staten Island, NY. I just passed the $1,000,000 mark in total revenue. Coming from a background with no tax experience to a million dollars in revenue has been an amazing journey. It is all due to the system and support that Liberty Tax offers to its franchise partners.

I Had No Business Experience

By Alex Davis/Zee, GA

I bought my first franchise from Liberty Tax seven years ago, and boy has it been an amazing journey. I was 23-year old young man with no business experience, or for that matter, any tax experience. I knew that I wanted to own my own business, but was unsure of what to do until I discovered Liberty. Over the last seven years, I have grown my business to eighteen locations. Liberty has given me an opportunity to learn how to run a business with a proven system and has forever changed my life.

My Fanatical Story

By Leo Feldmann/Marketing and Student of Liberty - Dry Ridge, KY

I am 22 years old and a 2014 Graduate of the University of Kentucky. I received my degrees in Accounting and Economics from UK Gatton Business School. I am enrolled in the fall semester to begin the Master's program in Accounting and then test for CPA exam in the summer of 2015.

My parents joined the Liberty Tax team in 2006. My brother and I immediately became marketing specialists and office staff. I was 14 and my brother was 12 years old. My parents have been coming to the Liberty Tax conventions for eight years. They insisted that my brother and I participate in the activities, which the convention staff had planned for convention goers. For seven years, we went on the "fishing trip", which is a story in itself. However, we never missed the keynote speakers in the opening session nor the special achievements awards won by franchisees. It was a very exciting time!!!

My parents also thought it important for my brother and me to sit in on a few breakout sessions of our choices. My brother chose Marketing and I chose the "Granddaddy of Tax Preparation." My first year, I listened to 5 straight sessions of Mr. John Hewitt, CEO. And every year since, I have been the little kid in the front row. Do you know how much a young boy can learn from 5 sessions, multiplied by 7 years???? Bunches!!! I listened to the pros and cons of the tax industry, how he delivered his message to fellow franchisees, his personal reflections on issues and how to handle questions, good and bad. I developed a sincere admiration for Mr. Hewitt. He made "sense" to me, and therefore I became focused on the same ideas and future of business concepts.

When Liberty Tax went public, I was thrilled because I understood the importance of such a venture. What an exciting time to be part of the Liberty Tax family. Now, here I am, eight years later in 2014, with an internship with Ashland Oil at the World Headquarters in Lexington, KY in the Tax Department. Thank You, Mr. Hewitt.

LIBERTY TOOK A CHANCE ON ME

LIBERTY TOOK A CHANCE ON ME

A Business Owner at Age 19!

By Jesus Rivas/Zee - Allentown, PA
(Liberty's Youngest Zee to Date)

I was raised by a single mother. We moved around a lot in my early years: New York, New Jersey, Nevada, Florida, Colorado, and finally Allentown, Pennsylvania. My mother is a hardworking woman, but never made a lot of money. There were times when we struggled a lot, but we were always all right.

At a young age, I found myself disinterested in most of the things my teachers had to say about making a living in this world. A lot of things they said never added up to happiness or an outcome I was content with. I found myself in high school getting my education from Napoleon Hill, Robert Kiyosaki, Tim Ferris, and websites like Forbes and Investopedia. I figured, I would get the same outcome as whoever's advice as I took. I often lived by the saying "Don't take advice from someone you would not want to trade places with."

At age 18, I graduated from high school (class of 2012), still not knowing what exactly I wanted to do, but knowing I wanted to make a difference in this world and have a good time doing it. As Will Smith once said "If you're not making someone else's life better, you're wasting your time."

I decided in order to be happy with my career choice, I'd have to write down a detailed list of what I'd like my life to be like and try to find a business or career that fit those standards. As you probably know, most people do the opposite. They find a career and mold their life to fit that career. After writing my list, I decided the tax business was perfect for the life I wanted to live!

I immediately signed up for the H&R Block course with a down payment of $50 to hold my spot. A month later, the instructor emailed me and said the class was being cancelled because I was the only one who signed up. I was extremely disappointed, but it turned out to be blessings in disguise. As I read the email about the class being cancelled, I was on the phone with a friend. I told her about the situation AND she immediately explained that she'd seen a sign for a free tax school at the Liberty Tax across town. I signed up for the course right away!

I was immediately drawn in by the culture of Liberty. I had seen Liberty in the "Forbes Top 20 Franchises for the Buck" list, so I knew there was something special going on in this company. I immediately began asking the owner of the store about the opportunity. He answered all my questions and I signed up for more information.

The very next day, I received a phone call from John Taylor (in Franchise Development) who I later found out was the 8th person involved with the company. We spoke for about 10 minutes. I was extremely excited! Then reality hit me and I said, "John, you know I'm only 18, right? He said, "Let me tell you something, ask me how old I am."

"How old are you?" I said. He said, "I'm 58. Last year, I was 57 and the oldest man to try out for the Olympics, so don't tell me anything about age. Stereotypes go both ways. I used to have guys your age working with nuclear weapons on submarines."

There's a saying that goes, "The only thing stopping you from having something is the story you tell yourself about why you can't have it." From that point on my excuse wasn't valid. I let it go.

John and I went back and forth for a couple weeks. He would tell me don't worry about the end product, just think about the next step. We spoke frequently. He recommended a few books to me and I read them right away. Tax season was also in full swing at this point and I'd been hired as a tax preparer. He then invited me to come down to Virginia Beach for 3 days for a discovery weekend. I was extremely excited!

At this point I already knew this was what I wanted to do. I had no idea how I was going to make it happen though. I had done all the research and learned everything I could about Liberty Tax Service, John Hewitt, and the tax industry.

While down in Virginia Beach, we had a meeting with John Hewitt at the convention center. I distinctly remember John Taylor coming up to me beforehand and saying, "I want you to sit right in the front. Your goal, at the end of this, is to make sure John Hewitt knows your name."

John Hewitt entered, we introduced ourselves and he spoke for a bit. He asked the prospective franchisees several questions. The first one was, "There are three certainties in life: death, taxes and does anyone know the third one?" I raised my hand. "Change?" I said, "Wow, how did you know that?" He said. (I'd watched a ton of his interviews and spoke with many of his corporate staff, so this was an easy one for me.)

His second question was, "Does anyone know what percentage of returns H&R Block does in this country?" Nobody knew. I raised my hand. "18%?" I said, unsure of my memory. "Wow! This 18 year old has all the answers," said John.

He also asked, "Does anyone know why someone starts a return with us and doesn't finish it?" Someone raised their hand and said, "The price?" That was incorrect. I raised my hand and said, "The refund amount!" I remember thinking to myself at this point everyone in the room was either impressed, or skeptical. But I was just happy to be there!

I returned home more excited than ever; I was saving every penny to make this dream a reality, but I still had no idea how I was going to make it happen. I attended training in April, still not completely sure how I was going to own a store, but deep inside of me I knew it was going to happen. I never had a single doubt. I didn't know how, but I knew that it would all work out, the same way that you know your name or that the sun is coming up tomorrow. That is how strongly and certain I knew that I would make this happen.

After returning home, I spoke with the owner of the store where I had previously worked. He had three stores and was a second year Zee. He offered to sit down with me and discuss selling me one of his stores. He decided to sell in Allentown and buy closer to his home in Lancaster, PA. I decided to buy his Hamilton Street store in Allentown. After going through training, I knew I could really turn things around there and make that office a superstar! We decided on a sales price and the down payment. The only problem was coming up with the money for the down payment.

I decided to try to get a loan. I made a business plan and went bank to the bank in hopes of making it happen, but nothing was going through, despite the loan officers saying they had never seen anyone so prepared, especially at my age. I refused to give in! I decided to sit down and renegotiate. As outrageous and unlikely as it sounds, we worked out a great deal for zero down. I think it was in part because he saw how badly I wanted this and admired my drive. We signed in July of 2013! I was officially a business owner at age 19, and one of my dreams had already come true.

I spent the off-season learning everything I could about running a successful store. I listened to every conference call I could, and read as much as possible about this business. I knew I had one shot at this. My back was against the wall. If I didn't do well this season, it would all be over as quickly as it started. It's amazing what one can accomplish when the stakes are so high.

Halfway through February, we were up 36% in tax returns! It has been surreal up until this point, and I am extremely humbled and thankful every day. I've had a lot of support from all the good people at Liberty and John Hewitt himself. I owe a lot to this company, and I am extremely loyal as a result of the opportunity they have given me. What other company would give me a chance to be in business for myself at 19 years old, with no college degree, and not a lot of life or business experience?

I've always thought of my inexperience as a blessing throughout this journey. I mean, think about it. I just do what John Hewitt tells us as best I can. Follow the system and succeed, no matter what age you are!

Life, LIBERTY, and the Pursuit of Happiness

By Diane Wagner/Area Developer - RI

I met John Hewitt between flights at an airport and inquired about a Jackson Hewitt Franchise. That brief meeting changed my life and the lives of my children. He took a chance on me and his confidence pushed me to begin a new chapter in my life and embark on a wonderful journey.

I followed John to LIBERTY in 2005, and continued to learn and to break new boundaries. I feel that God provided the perseverance, which was the key ingredient to achieving my goals. I am thankful for that and He used John to open a door.

Always goal oriented, and a generous teacher, John taught me how to serve clients, employees, and to grow as a businesswoman. Now, as a financially successful area developer for Rhode Island, and a confident person, I have, with John's help, launched my children on successful careers with LIBERTY. My daughter, Haley, is a franchise owner, and Heather is director of new company initiatives. For our family, LIBERTY continues to empower our pursuit of happiness.

Liberty Changed My Life Forever!

By Nancy Simonsen/Corporate Office Manager - Liberty Corporate

Fourteen years ago, I was a displaced Navy ex-spouse, single parent. I had plenty of experience in my home state, but hadn't been in Virginia that long. Mary Jane (DeJaager – Operations) and John took a chance on me. I didn't have much on-the-job training, so had to "wing it" at times. Especially on how to handle customers.

There were no manuals on how to do the job. As the company grew, so did my department. I had to create a manual, having learned most of it by personal experience. I wanted the department to have the knowledge and tools at their fingertips – with the manual, and now our department site. Liberty gave me the freedom to be creative, to find ways for us to improve and grow. I've never had that before.

As an education/psychology major in college, I have always had the desire to help others and to teach. This job is exactly that. We help the customers, franchisees, area developers, and fellow employees. Training in our department is constant, as things are always changing within the company.

Maintaining the Liberty culture is a challenge as we grow. Our Liberty "family," is still the best there is! We are always there for each other. My Liberty family makes me want to give 200% +. The employees under me want to give 200% +. I think it can't get any better than this! (But it will!)

Liberty has changed my life forever!

Liberty Gave Me a Chance

By Tim Ford/Technical Support - Liberty Corporate

My name is Tim Ford and I got my first start with Liberty in Spring Hill, Florida where I live. I am a self-employed I.T. tech. The mom of a friend of mine opened a Liberty tax office here in town and hired me to setup her computers. From time to time, she would call me to fix issues with Liberty's software.

As I became more familiar with the software, I decided to contact the Liberty Corporate office to see if they had any job opportunities. In November of 2008, I received a call from Leah Bryant at the corporate office. She asked me if I was interested in performing technical audits for new franchises in Florida. I enjoyed traveling around and helping new Zee's set-up their offices. Leah recommended me for a big tech job in Chattanooga, Tennessee. The following season, I returned as a tech auditor, only this time I got to do it remotely from home.

In 2010, I attended the Liberty convention and met Doug Granger. He told me he had heard good things about me and decided to give me a try as a remote tech support rep. That December, I received a phone call from Larry Johnson. The company flew me to Virginia for a week of training then I came home and did tech audits and support. Liberty was the first company to give me a chance to do what I am good at - providing technical support. I also love doing the tech audits.

I enjoy helping new franchisees. I check their systems to make sure they are correct and I teach and tutor them in the basics of using the Liberty software and website. It has been a gratifying experience and I have learned new skills. The most gratifying thing of all is when I get that call each year asking me if I would like to come back.

Liberty Showed up at the Perfect Time

Anonymous - Liberty Corporate

My new job came at the perfect time. I was in week fourteen of sixteen for my unemployment benefits, and the economic outlook for my wife and I was grim.

These are indeed challenging times for many people in terms of jobs, financcs, and savings (whether for emergencies, school tuition, or retirement). The issues impacting my family began many years ago when I was injured in a non-work-related accident. Under doctor's orders, I was required to take some time off of work to heal and recover. That is the tricky part, when two income families are living paycheck to paycheck, and the unexpected happens!

Now, we have two grown children and several grandchildren. There but for the grace of God goes my family, and working at Liberty Tax Service reminds me to count my blessings every day.

John Hewitt Believed in Me

By Sue Wickham/National Site Selection Director - Liberty Corporate

"A mentor is someone who sees more talent and ability within you, than you see in yourself, and helps bring it out of you." (Bob Proctor - Author, Speaker and Success Coach) For me, that mentor has been John Hewitt.

The year was 1987; my youngest child was starting junior high. As the mother of four teenagers, I was ready to pursue my dream of being a high school English teacher, a goal that I had given up to marry at 18, just weeks after graduation. It turned out to be the right decision, as we will be celebrating our 47th wedding anniversary on July 1st. My husband, Paul, worked as a machinist at Oneida Limited, in Sherrill, New York and with four growing mouths to feed we could not afford to send me to a four year college, so I started out at a two year school: Bryant and Stratton in a mall in Syracuse, where a Jackson Hewitt Tax Service had opened an office right around the same time as I started school.

I was having the time of my life! Here I was, 38 years old – by far the oldest student in my classes – and loving it! Alas, money issues were always rearing their ugly heads, and I went to the guidance counselor to see if there were any part time jobs available. That is when the "journey began" that was to change my life forever. I went to work part-time at Jackson Hewitt doing everything from receptionist to bookkeeper, processor, and janitor. Whatever needed to be done, I did it.

When tax season was over, I was hoping that they would hire me back for the following tax season and I planned on taking the fall tax class and becoming a tax preparer. However, as we all know, things happen that we never planned on and in July, Paul got hurt very seriously at work. We knew it was going to be a permanent injury and our roles were going to be reversed, I was going to have to leave school and become the "bread winner." The first thing I did after letting the school know was to go see my good friend, the manager of the Jackson Hewitt office and let her know what had happened. She told me to "hang in there" for a while that she may have something for me.

Well, to make a VERY LONG STORY SHORT, a few months later I find myself in a hotel training room in Virginia Beach learning how to be a general manager for Jackson Hewitt. I was one of a group of eight; six of them were businessmen in suits and a woman who had been in the tax business for years. Talk about feeling out of place! I had never flown in a plane or stayed in a hotel room by myself, never eaten a meal alone, had no clothing that was suitable for the training except for a blue suit with a blue and white blouse that I got on sale at JCPenney. To say that I felt like a fish out of water is an understatement, but I finished the training and got a message that John Hewitt himself wanted to see me in his office! Talk about scared. I had no idea what he was going to say to me. I was hoping he would offer me a job at the office in Syracuse, helping to manage it or another office close by. That was not to be.

He started out by asking, "Do you want to take the general manager job in Oakland, California or Kansas City?" Huh? I have children, a husband, and a life in upstate New York. I was stunned as I left his office I had no idea what I was going to do. Well, I chose Kansas City and on my way out of the office asked John," By the way, what do they eat in Kansas City?" And John responded," Kansas City strip steak of course." After peak season, they closed down the five Montgomery Ward stores that I was managing and once again, I got to decide, do you want to go to Chicago and work there or do you want to go home to New York and work in Syracuse? I responded, "Where do you need me the most?" I found myself in the "Windy City." What a first year of my new career!

Now, all of these years later, I am the National Site Selector for Liberty Tax. Along the way, I was a general manager for two of the largest franchisees at Jackson Hewitt. I owned offices in Georgia and Florida as a Jackson Hewitt franchisee, won numerous awards, and when John left Jackson Hewitt so did my passion and love of the business. My oldest daughter, Kelly, had already left her position there and was working for Liberty Tax, so I called John and asked to meet with him. He offered me a position with Liberty. It has been a great experience. I have held different roles here, starting at what is now a corporate area developer, running the sales department for a year before knowing that it was not, as John would put it, "playing to my strengths," and I went back to being a corporate AD. When we decided to bring site selection in-house, I was asked to take on the position that I currently hold. I love this company more than I could ever put into words.

How was any of this possible? I was a housewife and mother from a small city in upstate New York. I knew nothing about the tax business, I had no idea how to manage or own a business. It happened because a man named John Hewitt believed in me much more than I ever believed in myself. He gave me the opportunity to prove it and to change my life forever. Every step of the journey, through the highs and lows, the good and the bad, he was always there for me and I will be eternally grateful.

There is a P.S. to the story....

By the way, the dream of being a teacher was fulfilled, as I have taught site selection to our new franchisees in Basic Class and I also get the privilege of working with the new area developers coming into the system on both site selection and DMA meetings. As it turned out, John didn't only give me a career, but also two of my daughters, Kelly and Kathy, who have both worked at both of his companies for over 20 years.

"You Have a Way with People"

By Toni Smith/formerly Sales and Marketing - NM

I had been unemployed since 2007, and needed to get back in the work force. I saw an ad for the Liberty Tax class, so I called and spoke with Kim Pierce (Zee, New Mexico). This was January of 2012. I had no work experience for a few years and needed a chance. Kim gave me that chance.

I took the class twice a day with our teacher, Robb Biggs. I was having such a hard time getting it. I had worked in the medical field for years, so dealing with numbers or even sitting behind a desk was uncomfortable to me. Kim noticed right away that I was struggling, and she had a marketing position open.

One afternoon, she said to me, "You have a way with people, and I need a marketer." That afternoon, Kim and I went out in full Liberty fashion. She showed me her territory and what she expected from her marketing people. Right away, I fell in love with marketing.

I found a new path and this path led me to a full-time sales and marketing position right after tax season. Within a few months, the new company wanted me to relocate, but I couldn't. I started a new job search and found this amazing bank. I started with First Convenience Bank on August 20, 2012. Due to the education, confidence, and that push from Kim Pierce, I have now been promoted to assistant branch manager.

I know without the Liberty Tax family, my story would not be the same.

"When You Are a Millionaire, You Can Pay for Dinner"

By Sandy Stow/VP of Area Development - Liberty Corporate

In 2001, I was an optician and worked part time, making about $35,000 per year.

A friend of mine, Melissa Salyer (Franchise Development), introduced me to John Hewitt. She wanted me to open up a franchise with her, but I didn't know anything about franchises, or even taxes. I went to a seminar with Melissa, and John invited us out to dinner. He said, "I'll tell you what, why don't you come to work for me?" I had been in the same job for 16 years, but John said he would guarantee my salary for a year. If it didn't work out, I could always go back to being an optician.

My biggest concern was our daughter, Katie. She was 9-years-old and I didn't want to put her in daycare. So John said, "What if we put a desk for her in your office, and we can have the bus drop her off here. Your husband can swing by later, because he gets off of work before you do. He can pick her up and go home, and when you're off, you're off." I said yes.

Katie grew up at Liberty, with her own desk. A few times, she would go to John's office and say, "Mr. John, my mom is busy. Can you help me with my homework?" He always did. He would also write extra addition problems for her on my office white board.

My first year, I did really well as a sales representative. I contribute that to the fact that my mom, my dad, and my aunt were so pro-Liberty. My parents are very conservative with their money, but had watched Jackson Hewitt grow. My dad said that he wished he had been able to invest. On joining Liberty, Dad said, "Very rarely do people get opportunities like this." My parent's strong belief in John Hewitt and Liberty fueled my sales success.

I got my first commission check and didn't want to lose it by investing poorly. I asked if John would go out to dinner with my husband and me to discuss how to best invest my money. We talked about goals, which weren't very lofty, like paying for college. At dinner, the check came and I reached for it because I had invited John to dinner. He said, "Absolutely not! I'll tell you what, when you're a millionaire you can buy me dinner." I never forgot that.

My next goal was to become an Area Developer. I went to talk to John about this and he said, "Okay, you need a partner. Let me think about that." A couple of days later, he told me about a potential partner, a franchisee in Arizona. John believed we would make a good team and that we should partner in the Las Vegas region. He never gives reasons why. I said, "But, John, I was thinking of Miami."

He said, "Sandy, are you going to but me, or are you going to do what I say?" John's choice, Geoff Knapp, turned out to be a successful partnership. I had never even met him and we agreed to partner on the phone, because of John's belief in us. Geoff and I had no money and we were being 100% financed. I was buying an area worth more than my house. Once again, following John's system, we were very successful.

I went on to expand as an Area Developer in Dallas a few years later. As we were filling out loan papers, with assets and liabilities, I wrote down the numbers and couldn't believe it. I was a millionaire! I didn't even know it until then. I went and showed John and said, "I'm a millionaire, I get to take you to dinner."

John is also a practical jokester. He had been to the restaurant he selected the night before. Without me knowing, he conspired with the waiter to pretend to order two $400 bottles of wine. It turned out to be just $40 bottles, but I wouldn't have cared either way. No amount of money can match how much John and Liberty have changed my life.

When I first arrived at Liberty, I didn't know what the heck I was doing. I didn't even understand what a franchise was. I never dreamed this would be my life now. You don't have to be a rocket scientist; you just need the desire to succeed. My life – our daughter's life – will never be the same.

Check, please.

Thanks for Giving Me a Chance

By Edward Bryant/Liberty Product Support - JTH Financial

Liberty Tax Service has been a place that gives me a chance to learn new skills and find new talent inside myself. I am a handyman in the daytime, a musician at night, as well as a proud father of three kids, who are all straight A students. 2014 has been the coldest winter in over ten years. Before coming to work for Liberty Tax Service-JTH Financial, my job as a handyman was at its worst. Digging holes for pipes in the frozen ground was a back-buster and I wanted to come in from the cold and find a job working indoors.

A friend told me how happy they were working at Liberty as a customer service rep for two years. They told me that the company would train me and I would have flexible hours. I have long dreadlocks, no skills with computers, but the lovely team at JTH Financial treated me very nicely and helped me step-by-step.

When the calls started coming in, back-to-back, it was mind blowing. I had never worked in a call center before, however the supervisors were right there to help me out. Now we are at the end of the tax season and I am sad to let it go. Spring is here and Liberty Tax Service helped me make money, gain new skills, and kept me in a great indoor job in one of the coldest winters the East Coast has seen in many years.

I can't wait to work the phones and service the people that call in for Liberty Product Support. I know that I am part of the Liberty Tax family. Thanks for giving me a chance. I will be forever grateful.

Liberty Has Given Me a Sense of Pride

By Rachel A. Poulin/Franchise Development - Liberty Corporate

Let me start by saying that I come from a very modest home. A single, military mother of two raised me and although she worked hard, it was always more than a little rough financially. Despite the hard times, my mother always seemed to keep a roof over our heads and food on the table, but we never had any excess of anything. I have to say that although she had limited time, she was able to convey to us the importance of self-respect, hard work, and the fruition of success.

I worked hard in school, attended Old Dominion University for 4 years studying English and Journalism, while holding down 2 jobs and supporting myself through college. I have always had a job and have been working since the age of 15. My working career was always the same story; I was given the most responsibility, but never financially rewarded for my efforts. Nonetheless, I have always remained positive and driven, like my mother instilled in us.

I was introduced to Liberty Tax Service in 2007, and later became a franchisee for 2 years. It was great timing after being a bit deflated in 2008. I had just closed my retail business after owning it for nearly 6 years. Like most small businesses, the recession hit my business hard and it was difficult to see my investment slip away. Liberty was like a new chance - a new beginning for my daughter and me. In 2009, I joined Liberty's Franchise Development Team and feel I finally have a career that I completely and truly love.

Being a part of Liberty's Franchise Development Team has given me a sense of pride, the ability to travel and see our country, a sense of teamwork, flexibility to enjoy life and my family, and the ability to work hard and actually see my financial and professional dreams come true. Not to mention, I have grown as a person - having gained knowledge through lessons from our leader, John Hewitt.

I am forever grateful to Liberty Tax Service.

I Grew Up at Liberty

By Patricia Old/Area Development Assistant - Liberty Corporate

I joined Liberty when I was 18 years old, and I feel like I've literally grown up here. That was six years ago and I was a very introverted person. I didn't feel comfortable speaking in front of groups. Even scribing (writing on a white board), I would get so nervous.

Working at Liberty, I've learned a lot about myself. My first job was in sales, so I had to make phone calls and speak to people. That helped me become more extroverted. I wasn't looking for a promotion, but a lady I respected, Mary Jane DeJaager (now Director of Seasonal Relationships - Operations), found me. She told me that Liberty managers admired my work ethic, and I was promoted to working with her division.

Mary Jane and I shared an office, and she became like a second mother to me. I was 21, and living on my own. She was a strong, female presence in my life. Mary Jane became a mentor and was very good at separating business and personal issues. I would come in with boy problems, and she would give me her life lessons. She would tell me that there are other fish in the sea - you're better than that! She taught me so much.

On the business side, I was dealing with a very difficult person and she taught me how to deal with it in a professional manner. I'm very emotional, but Mary Jane coached me through it.

John Hewitt has also been a positive influence in my life. Our CEO walks around in shorts and tee shirts. He really does have an open door policy. One day, I walked in to his office and asked him to buy Girl Scout cookies. He bought a box of each! I like that our CEO is so accessible. We are all working for a common goal and Liberty offers training to help us.

I then moved to another division, Area Development, where I can bring my personality into my job. I now feel comfortable speaking and scribing in front of groups. I feel like I've come full circle. I've grown up at Liberty and the best part is - I'm still having fun!

I Got My Big Break Through Liberty

By Stacey Crutcher/Marketing Manager - Miamisburg, OH

My decision to work from home came about after a long 4 years of being unemployed and previously going back to school to get my Associates in Applied Business, Web Design from Ohio Business College. After graduating in 2011, I was out of work, actively looking with no luck except holding down odd jobs or in between temporary contract jobs in residential sales and marketing management.

Fed up and frustrated, I decided to work from home to start earning my own residual income. Recently, in December of 2013, I decided to partner with a wonderful Direct Sales Co. that provides a broad range of infant organic unique children's gifts. My desire to become an e-consultant was a result of the mission of the company in helping women to become independent business owners by helping them become successful at building their business. Also, I fell in love with their earth friendly products. While launching "Stacey's Pollywally Doodle," I knew I was on a path towards self-development.

It was January when I got my big break taking on a seasonal position with Dayton South Liberty Tax Service as a Marketing Manager. While building B2B relationships in representing the Liberty Tax Service brand has given me all the tools necessary to affectively approach my own business in building ongoing relationships with others. My way of defining fanatical is taking that leap of faith in starting something new you've never done before. Because of my fanatical leap I just want to say thank you Liberty Tax for being there for me in helping me build my business!

Liberty Gave Me Hope

Irma Stephanie Almaguer/Marketing - Seguin, TX

I started working for Liberty Tax Service on January 6th 2013. Since I first walked in to fill out an application and ask about the Rapid Tax class, I have felt welcome and like there was finally a little hope in my life.

I am a college student and my schedule is a very tough one to work with at times, because it is a quarterly based school and every three months my schedule changes again. Liberty has been the first place willing to work with my crazy school schedule.

I don't have a boss and coworkers - I have another family - people I share my life with, ask for advice from and who talk to me. I had been out of a job for a year and a half, thinking I would never find a job to help me pay for school, and then Liberty opened their door. Liberty gave me hope to keep pursuing my goals. This year, I started doing marketing for a new location my owner opened, and it has given me more confidence and courage to face any challenge. Liberty has provided me with experience that I know will help me in the future. I will always come back to Liberty every season to see my family and all the customers/friends I've made while working with Liberty.

Thank You for Giving Me My Life and Self-Esteem Back

Tammy Dunnuck/Tax Preparer - Abilene, TX

I had been married for almost 13 years to a man that had taken all of my self-esteem. He left me with two small children. I was just starting my business of being a nail tech, which I did for over 20 years. I did meet a wonderful man, and married him and we had a beautiful baby.

The longer I did nails, the less I enjoyed it and really wanted a new direction in my life. I started looking for other employment to no avail, so I started losing my self-esteem that I had gotten back through my new life. I really enjoyed doing our taxes, so I decided to take the Liberty Tax course, just to learn more about taxes. After the course, one of the owners of this franchise asked if I would work for them. I thought and prayed about the offer and returned with a yes.

I have only worked as a tax professional this season, but feel that it has changed my life forever. The owners of this franchise gave me a chance when no one else would. I was really so down on myself, with no self-esteem any longer. They have now given me my self-esteem back and I want to do so much for them. They have also talked to me about other opportunities for the future and I look forward to whatever they have in store for me. I am so happy that I was given this chance and it is because of Liberty Tax Service and the franchise owners that you have. Thank you, so much, for giving me my life and self-esteem back.

Liberty is the Better Job!

By Jacqueline Sadler/Employee - East Liverpool, OH

I was desperately looking for a job, any job, when I came upon an ad online for jobs at Liberty. I thought it would be just a job to get me through until I could find a better job, but little did I know this was the better job.

I just love working for Liberty. It is a great opportunity to meet people in my community, make new friends, and work with some great people! Not only is it income for me, but I also know there is room for advancement and growth. This is exactly what I was looking for in a job - not a job - but a career.

I am very excited with the prospect of returning next year and I am looking into advancing my education to be better equipped in helping others get the best possible help with their tax returns. Thanks Liberty!!!

I'm Never Going Back to Manual Labor

Rico Hamilton/First Year Zee, Tax Support - Hampton Roads, VA

I went to college to study accounting but worked for six years in manual labor jobs, before completing my bachelor's degree in 2012. It was easy to get these jobs, working in shipyards or temporary employment for $9/hour. My community supported me and lifted me up when I felt like I was at the bottom, and I knew I wanted to transition from manual labor to being a thinker. This became my motivation.

In September of 2013, I saw an ad for Liberty Tax on Craigslist and interviewed for a tax preparer position. The District Manager, Margie Finneran, saw something in me beyond what was being offered. She asked me if I was interested in the Office Supervisor position. I had never run a store and this was my first big professional opportunity.

I studied hard and focused. Because I understand taxes, Margie put me in charge of teaching Tax School, which gave me the chance to work on public speaking. This was my first time teaching and with every class, I felt my confidence growing. Each session became more fun. People were ready to come to class - with smiles on their faces. My experience with Liberty was a complete success. I worked hard, followed John Hewitt's Top Ten (principles for success) and, overall, we grew in revenue by 31% from the previous year.

It's also great to have a CEO with a winner's attitude; that was my first impression of him. John has gained my respect as a businessperson. We fought off a competitor trying to steal our customers and John didn't back down. I was impressed by the structure of the corporation, based upon winning straight from the top. As the tax season ended, I thought my winning season may be coming to an end, but Liberty Corporate offered me a job in tax support. They saw something in me and I am working on revising our franchisee tax schoolbook to make sure it's in compliance with new tax laws.

The blessings didn't stop there. I've learned that growth comes in being able to accomplish tasks set aside for certain individuals. This isn't something just anyone can walk in and do. Luck is opportunity plus preparation. John noticed the growth at just one store and offered to have a lunch meeting with me. I had never sat down and talked with a person who has had so much influence and success at what he does. To say I was nervous was an understatement. As an athlete in high school, my coach told me that it's okay to have pre-game jitters, but if you're nervous during the game, you're just scared. I spoke honestly and John was genuinely interested in me. He asked a lot of questions about me and there was no intimidation. John offered me the opportunity and support to become a franchisee and this year I will begin my life as a business owner. How can I fail with someone who has started an empire? I trust his experience and I'm extremely confident going into this season.

With so much pressure and capital on the line, I don't feel any fear. I understand financials, accounting, database management and this is an opportunity of a lifetime. I did my research, but found the best way to make a good decision was to ask John. I have big plans and will never go back to my old life. I have become the motivation for a lot of youth in my community. I would love to invest in things that will make a difference. Liberty has given me that opportunity. Now, if I do manual labor (landscaping for my family) I do it because I want to - as a way to give back - not because I have to.

The Path to Liberty!

By Heather Smith/Corporate Director and former Zee

I am a rebel by nature – born that way, I guess. My mother, Diane Wagner, loved taxes from the time I was a really young girl. She started at H&R Block where pen and paper were still used and smokers were plenty in the offices!

I had no interest in taxes or being in the tax business. My younger sister, Top Gun B Franchisee, Haley Klein, went to college and graduated with an accounting degree, I think! She worked with my mother through college at her Jackson Hewitt location. She was destined. I, on the other hand, decided to travel and move to different cities on both U.S. Coasts.

I became pregnant in 2003 and decided it was time to develop a skill or find a career. I took my first fall tax school at my mother's Jackson Hewitt location at 26 years old. I did so-so in the class and was semi-interested. That January, John Hewitt provided me with my first opportunity, to assist in opening and marketing 5 locations in Cleveland, OH. AD, Fred Bobel, also came to work with us there and is still an AD today.

I had my daughter April 27th, 2004, just after that tax season. I took the summer off with her and worked with Haley that fall and tax season, 2004-2005 at her Liberty Tax Service office in Fremont, OH.

I was married and divorced in 2004-2005 with a completely diminished bank account, so I moved in with my father who helped my daughter and me immensely. We had nothing and I didn't know how I was going to make a great life for her. Any single mother can relate to the fear of gaining a successful career and raising your child well…thinking both will never happen.

I worked in retail in 2005-2006 when I was given my 2nd opportunity by John Hewitt! I inquired about opening my own office and he financed my first office in the very small town of Zelienople, PA (population approximately 4,000). The following year, I acquired another location in Robinson Twp., PA. Both locations are in and around Pittsburgh. During the course of those couple of years, the corporate office was also contracting me to do software testing on our proprietary software. That led to me managing more than 50 other franchisees nationwide also testing the tax software.

After managing that group, I was asked to consider taking a permanent position in Virginia Beach with the corporate office. I was beyond thrilled and astounded that they really thought there was any value in me. The decision, however, was difficult because I had no friends and no family here. I only had the hope of a great future for my daughter.

It took me nearly a month to decide, but I eventually determined this was our best opportunity yet! Opportunity #3! I really never thought I was very smart or that I'd amount to much in life. I thought the best I could hope for was to be a really good administrative assistant.

We moved here in April 18, 2008 and I reported to work on April 21st. I became the Director of Tax School, a position I enjoyed. I got to be involved in several other operational aspects that challenged me as well and were very fulfilling. I continued to run the Pittsburg area offices through 2009 when I determined it was too difficult as a single mom of a very young child to work full-time and run two offices remotely. In 2012, I became the Director of Guerrilla Marketing and I was over the moon! I know the company's success was due in large part to this type of marketing and felt that this was a prestigious position to be able to take on! It was exciting and a great learning experience.

In Spring 2014, I was given the opportunity to work on new company initiatives, particularly with the Hispanic brand. Again, the learning experience alone is amazing! The challenge is something that I thrive on and couldn't be more excited about.

When it's all said and done, the opportunities created by Liberty, by John Hewitt, have forever changed my life. No matter where I am or where I go, it's these opportunities that have made all the difference for me and for my daughter! I didn't think I had much intelligence or could bring value to a company. I was broke and had to care for my child. Nothing mattered or does matter to me more than providing a good life for her. It was tough on us moving here, but I have no regrets! These opportunities make it possible for me to do exactly what I want for her – give her a good life! And not only that, but I have found value in my intelligence, my creativity, and myself. I know my worth and I have John to thank for that.

I'm not very good at expressing these types of feelings and would prefer not to. But, I think it's important that people know just how much Liberty and John have changed my life and that of my daughter's and how they continue to do that for more people every single day!

I suppose I would also need to thank my mother for her taking a leap and opening a Jackson Hewitt location, which led us all down this path to Liberty!

University of Phoenix Scholarship Winner!

By Katrina Longan/Manager - Colorado Springs, CO

When I began working for Liberty Tax, I was pregnant and looking for a part time job that would ease the transition from working as a full-time server to a more relaxing office environment that would accommodate my growing belly! I invested a few dollars in myself to take the Rapid Tax Course because it would be an investment in a new skill that could potentially lead to employment. If I were not selected to be a part of the office, at least I would know how to file my taxes with the new baby on the way. I never expected to love the job so much! Since that class three years ago, I have worked my way up to office manager with a goal to own my own office in the future.

Every year, Liberty offers the University of Phoenix Scholarship and I remember hearing about it my first year but unable to qualify, I waited. The following year I was turned down for the scholarship, but after taking a few classes at the local college throughout the year, I re-applied with a bit more knowledge and received the scholarship. Hooray! Persistence pays off! Being awarded this scholarship relieves a huge financial burden for my family. My husband is in school as well, we both work, and we have a 2-year-old daughter whom we love to the moon and back. This scholarship is going to allow us to keep our student loan debt down, get us closer to home ownership, on my path towards becoming a Zee, and eventually the financial freedom to give my daughter the world. There are not enough words to describe the impact this will have on my family. I am grateful to work for a company that has an enthusiastic and supportive team with the ability to impact people and change lives on a daily basis.

I want to thank my awesome Zee, Tami Woestemeyer, for all of the experiences I have had this tax season. She put me in full force as a manager and by allowing me to experience all aspects of running an office from hiring to training, marketing and daily operations, I know that Liberty Tax is the company I want to center my career around. I know there is plenty that I can improve on, but Tami showed me that as long as you're consistently improving and adjusting, each tax season can and will be better than the last. I would also like to thank our wonderful staff this season. Without their upbeat personalities and encouraging words when I was stressed out about school, or working long hours at the office during Peak, or writing my scholarship essays, I probably wouldn't have made it through the season with my brain intact. Liberty means opportunity to me, and I can't wait to take full advantage of the educational opportunity Liberty Tax has provided to me through this scholarship! Some day I hope to influence somebody else's life the way Liberty Tax has influenced mine.

Winning a Full-Tuition Scholarship

By Abhinav Mehta/Tax Preparer - Defiance, Ohio

While I was in my junior year in college, I was becoming increasingly desperate because I still didn't know what I wanted to do when I graduated, and I didn't have any relevant accounting work experience to be able to find a good job. This is when I found an amazing opportunity with Liberty Tax that I won't ever forget.

In Defiance, the town where I lived and went to college, there was a new Liberty Tax office opening and the owner, Mary Geckle, was hiring tax preparers. Realizing how amazing an opportunity this was, I applied immediately, and was overjoyed when I was hired and trained. The work I was doing at the tax office was directly relevant to what I was learning in class in college, and I also realized the work experience was preparing me for a career after I graduated.

So I continued to work for Mary Geckle throughout the 2013 tax season as a tax preparer, and was hired again for this year's tax season. I also learned quite a bit from Mary directly during 10 weeks of tax training. This training, combined with the work experience, was brilliantly preparing me to become a knowledgeable tax professional.

Then a couple of months into the tax season, Mary sent me an email about a University of Phoenix full-tuition scholarship opportunity through Liberty Tax. Going to graduate school was one of my most important goals because it was essential if I wanted to become a CPA, but I was always worried about the cost. Again, I realized how amazing an opportunity this could be, so I applied immediately. Fast-forward a few months, and in May I received a call from Liberty Tax congratulating me on winning the full-tuition scholarship to the University of Phoenix!

I am still quite amazed at this perfect opportunity, and I can't thank Liberty Tax and the University of Phoenix enough for making this possible. I also must thank Mary Geckle, who gave me a wonderful job at the Liberty Tax office for two tax seasons and who informed me about this scholarship. I really am quite surprised how much my life has changed for the better since I've become involved with Liberty Tax Service.

A Scholarship Will Change My Life

By Andrea Zank/Zee - Chesapeake, VA

I was fortunate enough to be offered an opportunity to join the Liberty Tax team as a franchisee. Boy oh boy - has my life changed in the short nine months since then! This life changing chain of events has me on my way to financial freedom, more time with my children, and, best of all, success and flexibility to live my life how I want it lived.

Not only has Liberty Tax helped me to realize my dream of being a business owner, a partnership between Liberty Tax and University of Phoenix is about to help me realize my dream of earning my MBA. I'm the super blessed and incredibly lucky winner of one of the three full-tuition scholarships to University of Phoenix! This will change not only my life, but my children's lives as well.

I can't say enough how much this opportunity has meant to me. I'm so excited to be part of such a dynamic organization. The support is outstanding and I am going to work my hardest to be part of the team of franchisees who helps Liberty Tax to become the best and largest tax preparation organization in the universe!

LIBERTY BEYOND BORDERS

The Land of the Free

Mufeed Haddad/National Area Developer

When I first came to this country, I didn't know much about our business, but I knew how to develop networks and work with people. In the end, that's what every business is about. Everything I needed to know about tax preparation, I learned in the training program, Liberty College. The best thing about franchising is that it's a proven system. To be successful in any business, you must have good staff. You must empower them, hold them accountable, and pay them well. This is one of the major keys in developing a strong franchise.

I would highly suggest this business for other immigrants. There is so much to learn about doing business in a new country, and franchises reduce the pressure. If you follow the system and work hard, you'll be successful. This country really is the land of the free, a land of opportunity, and the greatest country in the world.

I would advise others to start following the system immediately! My partner and I were too complacent at the beginning of our experience with Liberty, thinking it was going to be easy. We thought that as long as we leased the right location and did the marketing, that the business would just happen. We thought we knew better than the experts, who developed the system, and it cost us two or three years of getting our business developed. That's what separates the top franchisees from the others – the ones that take it seriously and work hard to execute the system. So, don't be arrogant!

You have to understand that you will run into obstacles, and then learn to use them to develop your skills. Obstacles are a part of life, and you have to believe in yourself. You must be willing to rethink your strategy when things aren't going well. And then remain disciplined and ready to take action; you can't afford to get discouraged.

I've been so fortunate many times, by making the decision to come to the United States. I went through many disappointments and roadblocks just to get a visa, but it's a dream I had and I wanted to do it no matter what the price. And everything I went through was worth it. This Land of the Free can provide anybody and anyone with anything they can dream of, but it's going to be up to each person to figure out how to realize their dreams. People think it's going to be easy, but it doesn't work like that; you still must do the work!

Bringing Smiles to Children in Mexico

By Gilbert Mercado/Zee - Del Rio, TX

Our office is located in Del Rio, Texas on the U.S./Mexico border. For the past several years my wife, Irmarie Mercado, and I donate funds each year to Mrs. Carmen Rendon. These funds are used to provide children in our sister city in Mexico with toys, cake, and drinks in the traditional celebration of "Three Kings Day."

Although we cannot participate in the event due to the fact that it is held in Ciudad Acuna, Mexico, Mrs. Rendon provides us pictures and a video of the event each year. There are many children in our sister city that live in poverty and this event makes sure that hundreds of them will smile when they receive their gifts and sweets.

From Cleveland to Africa – Liberty Changes Lives!

By Veronica Ross/ Office Supervisor - Cleveland, OH

I am a company store employee; one day I will be a franchise owner. I will tell you how Liberty has changed my life and how it has changed the lives of others. I have been in the Cleveland, Ohio area for a couple years. I started running an office for a zee and then ran three of his offices. He sold to move and expand his territory, and I continued on as a corporate employee. I have since been able to build and sell two of the offices and now I am down to one office - the greatest out of the three - because I have changed a few lives.

I was fortunate to be able to teach over 121 students this year and two in particular touched my heart. One is a mother under thirty with three sets of twins, and pregnant again with another set of twins. She was struggling to get her GED and wanted so much to start a career. I was so amazed at her everyday struggle as a single mother (going to a GED class, and attending my class for ten weeks) that I had to present her with the Liberty Scholarship. She exceeded my class expectations, arriving two hours early every day despite such a hectic lifestyle. I was so excited when she took her test and earned a 97%. Those that teach know that doesn't happen often. She wanted to re-take the test to get 100%. She now works for Liberty as a tax preparer and she is aiming towards her Level 2. She has four sets of twins now and she is so glad that we took a chance on her. I feel I gave my Liberty Scholarship to the right person. She now works for us and is using her GED to attend college where she is studying tax law. She plans to one day own her own office, or four as she says.

The other client-turned tax student who has changed my life was a lady who came in after using Turbo Tax to do her personal, business, and non-profit group taxes, all in one tax return. What a mess! I must say that after about 30 hours of meetings to fix this, we developed a relationship that is non-stop. One of the many things that I learned about her is that she, like myself, is a veteran, has a home health nursing company (I also was in nursing), and she has a not-for-profit organization here in Cleveland called "Save A Teen". This organization not only targets the teens that are stuck in the circle of drugs and violence, but how it affects the family as a whole. She provides counseling to help revive nuclear families in dire situations.

I have provided a place to offer help for teenage mothers, teens who need a project to get them off the streets and a place for those who want to change their lives and start a career. We offer a drop-off for donations for school supplies and coats, gloves and hats to help people survive this brutal Cleveland winter that we are having. The teens come by and offer to clean-up and plant flowers and now that it is tax season, they are one of the several marketing groups I have started. Since this relationship has developed, they now know me as "Miss V" and are busy marketing in my territory with all the sticky notes I can supply. In return, we are giving a SAF to the organization of $25.00 for each new customer.

The most rewarding is the gift to Africa. I am fortunate that the office needed new computers this season. What a difference those old computers made! Liberty Tax donated those old computers to an organization that has been setting up schools in Africa. The founder of this organization is an extraordinary man who came to the United States as a refugee during the first Liberian civil war. He settled down in the Cleveland area and is now a successful entrepreneur and has raised a family here. He returned to his home village for the first time in twenty years in the late 2000's and found there to be no school in the entire Konobo District where he grew up. He returned on a mission to open a school in his hometown. That was realized last year when a K-12 school opened that services such a wide area that children now walk many miles to attend. Liberty donated computers and school supplies and clothing. We have now partnered by offering $25 SAF to new customers that are referred by the Dougbe River Presbyterian School c/o John Luttermoser.

Even though I am not a franchise owner yet, I have sent this message because Liberty Tax has made a difference in my life and in the people around me.

Giving at a New Level

Anonymous

One year, I prayed to God asking, "What do you want me to do to serve you?" The culture of giving at Liberty Tax encouraged us to feed the hungry in our own community and in the world. I set a huge goal. The numbers will stay between God and me, but I was able to donate more money that year than I had ever made in my life in a yearly salary, while I was in the military. That money went to feed starving people through Stop Hunger Now, founded by John Hewitt.

I can't wait to see what happens as we all work together to END world hunger through John's new organization, Run for Food International. The goal is huge – to solve this problem. From what I can tell, when you set a HUGE goal, God shows up.

Letter from Lee Warren

Community Relations Manager - Stop Hunger Now
(printed with her permission)

November 19, 2013

Dear John,

I joined Stop Hunger Now in 2006 to take the program into Virginia, yet we never had the opportunity to get to know each other. To get to the point immediately, I'm at the age in life where expressing gratitude is something I take more seriously than ever. When someone comes to mind, I make a point to contact them.

This past weekend during a long trail run, I was going over in my head a presentation I am to give in Pennsylvania this week about SHN. Since I always recount your contribution to co-founding SHN in my speeches, you came to mind, but in my solitude, with no distractions, I stopped my speech rehearsal and began to focus in on the gratitude I have for all that you allowed us to create.

Over 122 million meals in just about 8 years! As Ray Buchanan and our team were headed to the Philippines to work with our partners, not just to distribute the meals already on the water, but to set up an SHN packaging event (through Rotary) so Filipinos can help their own right in their own country, I was once again in awe of the power of one person, with a vision, to change the world. Then

one person became two people and now hundreds of thousands of people around the world know the privilege of contributing to the alleviation of hunger.

Thank you. Sincerely, thank you. You and Ray gave me the opportunity to live out a God-given purpose and you gave all of us a channel for good.

Sincerely,
Lee

Ending World Hunger One Country at a Time

By Chuck Lovelace/VP - Affordable Care Act
Run for Food International Co-Founder with John Hewitt

I've been associated with Liberty almost from the beginning. In those early years, I saw firsthand John Hewitt's passion and drive to eradicate hunger. I have to admit that I just didn't get it. I listened to the stories about the hungry children, but never made the connection that I could make a difference.

A few years ago, I had the opportunity to work with John on a project, as a consultant, where I saw firsthand how dramatic the hunger crisis is around the world. I was personally touched by the extreme need I saw around our globe.

After that experience, I was drawn to the desire to continue working with John to make a difference in this fight to end hunger. Run for Food International was started as an organization to recruit runners to help support this cause, but the name took on a much different meaning the day I saw children in Nicaragua, carrying empty bowls, literally running for food – rice with soy and vegetables. In many instances, that would be their only meal for the day.

Our goal isn't just to provide food for a day, but to teach communities to produce and grow food for a lifetime. Our mission is "to find innovative and sustainable solutions that will end world hunger." John's talent is to grow businesses and create systems, and his motivation is to use those resources to change the world.

Together, we chose Nicaragua as our first country in which to focus our efforts to eradicate hunger. With the help of our Liberty family, we will learn and grow, and take our system of solving hunger to other countries.

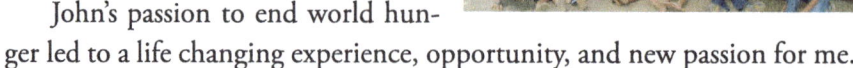

John's passion to end world hunger led to a life changing experience, opportunity, and new passion for me.

20/20 Vision

By Carolyn Castleberry/Director of Special Projects - Liberty Corporate

I joined Liberty Tax just six months ago after working most of my life as a business journalist, and the last couple of years as a financial advisor. I also have a heart for missions – helping to feed the hungry and helping vulnerable children. For many years, John was a guest on our newscast (I was one of the interviewers), but it wasn't until many years later, I learned that his passion is to SOLVE world hunger.

Along with Chuck Lovelace, we began working on a hunger project in Nicaragua with a man I will never forget, Oscar Corea. When I visited Oscar's village with a church ministry, I couldn't believe a place like this existed on this earth in this century. It is built on a garbage dump with a river of toxic, green water where the children play. I couldn't help but think of our own kids, in this country, who take clean water for granted by simply turning on a faucet. I also watched these children in Nicaragua sorting through the piles of trash for something – anything – to eat. Like John Hewitt, Oscar has a dream – to end hunger, starting with his small community. These are families with a desire for a better life and a spirit of perseverance. Sounds like some other people I know.

When I had the chance to join Liberty, I knew this was a company with a big heart, but I had no idea how big! I've read each of these stories for our first "Fanatical," book and I'm convinced that if any group of people can make a dent in the world hunger problem, it's Liberty. John is a brilliant strategist and hopes to use his business experience and success to create a sustainable model to end hunger around the globe. Yes, Liberty's 2020 vision is about winning. It's also about transforming lives in every community and saving lives around the world – one hungry child at a time. Now that's 20/20 vision!

Achieving My Dreams Through Liberty

Betsabe Gonzalez/Tax Preparer - Lumberton, NC

First and foremost, I started working with Liberty Tax Service in January of 2013. I started my ten-week course in October of 2012 in Fayetteville, North Carolina. I was very nervous, but confident at the same time. I knew something good would come out of this course. From the beginning, I was promised a job in Fayetteville and then, at the last minute, they me told they had enough preparers. I did not let this bring me down, so I applied at Liberty Tax Service in Lumberton, North Carolina. To my surprise they pretty much hired me on the spot. I was so happy - excited because I knew my hard work had paid off.

I remember starting the course and taking my five-month old son with me to class, because sometimes I did not have a sitter. I would find struggles and obstacles, but I finished the course and completed my first certification required to do tax returns. I was so happy and proud of myself for completing the course. After every class I would get home, just to study, so my next class I would be prepared for the next lesson. I had a great mentor by the name of Eileen. She was really good to me, believed in me, and helped me out a lot. My husband helped me out a lot also. He was so patient and would get my son when he wanted to get in the way, while I was studying or taking my certification exams. Surprisingly enough, I was also four months pregnant when I was trying to finish the course.

Liberty Tax Service has changed my life so much. I have met great people, mentors, and coworkers. My boss is such a great person who inspires me to believe above and beyond. I do not see her much because she manages five other franchise offices. When I do get to see her, I feel that she always motivates me to follow my dreams and continue advancing in my career. Last tax season, my office leader was Jackie Villafuerte. She is a good mentor and a great tax preparer who assisted me, as it was my first tax season. I had done taxes before, but I never worked for a tax company before. This was all new to me, but Jackie was patient with me. I always had lots of questions, but she would walk me through tax returns and made sure I knew what I was doing. I also came to know Ashley, who is now my office leader. Ashley is a very hard worker at what she does and is so sweet. She has also helped me in the leadership role and encourages confidence in those who don't believe they have it.

At Liberty Tax, I have learned more about how to serve my customers and how to be more attentive. I have built more confidence with them and now I know I will offer great customer service and the fun thing is meeting people and assisting them. Liberty Tax Service does just as their motto says they do: set the standard, whether it is going out of their way to help their customers, especially if it is just educating them. Liberty always loves to improve everyday, educating their preparers by constantly training them and, for sure, bringing their clients together for customer appreciation and throwing roadside parties to have fun.

I was recently invited by Liberty to go to Shallotte because the Mexican consulate from Raleigh, NC was going to be taking applications for passports. I was so amazed with the number of people who had shown up to get their passport. The Mexican consulate from Raleigh comes down periodically to offer their services for those who may not know how to get this done. Liberty's main purpose was not to sell a tax return, but to let them know that we would be available in revising past tax returns for free, that we do free consultations, and give free information about upcoming tax laws. Liberty offers free applications for those in need of an ITIN, Tax ID also known as a green social. We let people know that most of our services are free of charge. I felt very glad that I could be of assistance in this way in my community. My goal in life is to be of assistance to the Hispanic community and I feel that Liberty has been instrumental in helping me get where I want to be in life.

Thank You, Liberty Tax Service, for helping me achieve my dreams.

The Security to Believe in Me!

By Dominga Guajardo/ Tax Preparer - San Antonio, TX

Liberty gave me the opportunity to learn something new. It also gave me the security to believe in me. When I started with the classes to be a tax preparer, I wanted to give up. But my manager and the store owner believed in me and they didn't allow me to give up.

Now I have a job, knowledge, and attitude that helps me believe in me. Now I not only know how to prepare taxes, I also help the community. And getting involved in Una Familia Sin Frontera, I can help the Hispanic family. During the week of 10 February, I participated along with my manager in the Semana Financiera at the Mexican Consulate. Here we provided information about the ITIN and ACA.

I can only thank God and those around me who believe in me. Because, thanks to them, I discovered that everything I want to do, I can make it happen.

Join Our Family Business

By Danny Hewitt/A Co-founder of
Liberty Tax Service/Guerrilla Marketing Expert

Let's talk fanatical. I've traveled the world, 200 days per year, in a Liberty costume! Planes, trains, and automobiles – everywhere I went – football and basketball games. Our team even showed up at a Snoop Dog concert in Chico, California. I had 6 people in costume with me carrying big bags of Dum Dums (candy). They loved us!

One year, I flew into Chicago and brought about 2000 Statue of Liberty crowns to celebrate the 4th of July at a Cubs game. I had 15 people helping me when I received a text from one of our franchisees, asking if we were in town? I told him yes. He replied, "I can tell, I'm at the Cubs game!" You never know where we'll show up. We never stop having fun!

This journey started for me in 1997. Originally, I began writing technology with my dad, but I found my passion in marketing. Not just any marketing – Guerrilla Marketing. Our team implemented this strategy at Liberty, and I've personally lived it.

In 2006, we took Liberty to another fanatical level. We created a Culture Committee from all of the different departments. Our goal was to create a place where people would wake up and want to come to work. Many people spend more time with their co-workers than with their own families, so you want to be in a place that you love, a place where people love to help each other. We also wanted to create a culture where people would feel challenged and free to be innovative. At Liberty, you can always find a new place, a new city, or a new project to work on. If you want to learn and improve everyday, the opportunities are here. Just walk into a Liberty store and you can feel the difference immediately.

For entrepreneurs, there are thousands and thousands of franchises out there. How do you pick the right one? Another reason to pick Liberty is because you're going to have to kill us to stop us. Nobody is going to stop us! Our goal is to be the number one tax company in the universe by the year 2020. We all become the words that we speak. At Liberty, we state our goals every day. We are winners. We are going to be number one – no question.

We say it, live it, and drink it. Most of all, we believe it. That drive runs through all of us, from my father to our newest employees.

In this book, you have read the stories – Liberty is the company that can take someone from nothing to everything. So what does it take to be a Liberty Zee?

When my dad sold Jackson Hewitt, he didn't need any more money. We have created Liberty because we love it. We are looking for people who are hungry; who will strive to run their business better than anyone else. We don't care what you've done before or where you come from. If you're going to step into this arena, you better be ready to play ball. When we come to town, we are ready to win. We want to see wavers on the side of the road (I'll be out there dancing with them!), we will call every business owner and knock on every door we can. We also want owners who will provide second-to-none customer service, and give back to their communities in fanatical ways.

We want to read your story on our next pages. It's your turn. Liberty will help you write your new chapter to freedom when you join our family!

**Visit www.fanaticalatliberty.com
for more life-changing stories.**

a Book's Mind

Whether you want to purchase bulk copies of
Fanatical at Liberty
or buy another book for a friend, get it now at:
www.abooksmart.com

If you have a book that you would like to publish, contact Floyd Orfield, Publisher, at A Book's Mind: floyd@abooksmind.com.

www.abooksmind.com

CPSIA information can be obtained at www.ICGtesting.com
Printed in the USA
BVOW11s0345041114

372952BV00001B/1/P